CONTENTS

KT-504-827

THE TUDOR AGE

THE TUDOR AGE REPRESENTS a pivotal period in English history. In little more than a century the nation was transformed from a medieval kingdom into an emergent modern state, on the brink of becoming a major world power. The change began when Henry Tudor, a virtually unknown Welshman, asserted his rival claim to the English throne and defeated Richard III at the Battle of Bosworth. Lasting just a few hours on a summer's afternoon in 1485, this was a minor battle but one that had major consequences. Richard III was killed in the fighting and Henry Tudor seized the English Crown. Thus was established a dynamic new dynasty that was to have a huge impact on England's future.

The Tudor rulers, like their medieval predecessors, were convinced that they could govern their subjects using whatever methods they considered appropriate.

A ROYAL FAMILY

Henry VIII seated on his throne with his son and heir, Prince Edward, at his right hand and his beloved Jane Seymour on his left. Princess Mary stands on the left of the painting, Princess Elizabeth on the right.

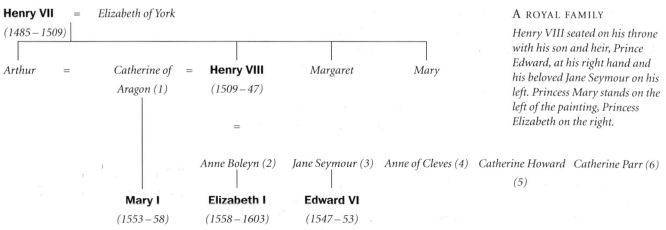

| **Henry VII** | = | *Elizabeth of York* | | | |
| (1485 – 1509) | | | | | |

| *Arthur* | = | *Catherine of Aragon (1)* | = | **Henry VIII** (1509 – 47) | *Margaret* | *Mary* |

=

| | *Anne Boleyn (2)* | *Jane Seymour (3)* | *Anne of Cleves (4)* | *Catherine Howard (5)* | *Catherine Parr (6)* |

| **Mary I** (1553 – 58) | **Elizabeth I** (1558 – 1603) | **Edward VI** (1547 – 53) |

Search all corners

of the earth to find

TUDOR ENGLAND

PETER BRIMACOMBE

world for pleasant

fruit and princely

delicates.'

Publication in this form copyright © Jarrold Publishing 2004, latest reprint 2006.
Text copyright © Jarrold Publishing.
The moral right of the author has been asserted.
Series editor Angela Royston.
Edited by Angela Royston and Ruth Midgley.
Designed by Simon Borrough.
Picture research by Jan Kean.

The photographs are reproduced by kind permission of: AKG, London 72, 77b, 80l & r, 81t; Ashmolean Museum, Oxford 75r; The Blair Castle Collection, Perthshire 51t; The Board of Trustees of the Armouries 14t (II.5. VI.1–5), 15t, 27b (VII.4, VII.147, V.79); Bodleian Library 44l, 57c, 65l, 70tl; Bridgeman Art Library 7t (British Museum), 10l, 12, 18b, 19, 20t, 22, 27c, 28t, 30, 31l & r, 33b, 34r, 37r, 51b (detail) (Scottish National Portrait Gallery), 55t, 66b (Private Collection), 67r, 71l (Fitzwilliam Museum, Cambridge), 71t, 70/71 (Private Collection/The Stapleton Collection), 74, 78b & 79 (British Library), 81b (Barber's Hall), 83t (British Library), 86, 87t (Private Collection), 87b (British Library); Peter Brimacombe 46b, 53b, 55b, 66t, 67l, 85t & br; British Library 7b, 36, 45b, 50, 65t, 69t, 70tr, 73b, 75l, 78t; British Museum 33t, 40t, 53t, 54t; Collections 32 (John D. Beldom); The College of Arms 13t, 61t & b; The Master and Fellows of Corpus Christi College, Cambridge 88; Crown Copyright 39tr; Dean and Chapter of Windsor 23t; Dean and Chapter of Westminster 39bl; DoE 45t; Edinburgh University Library 83b; English Heritage 25t, 26, 27t, 43l; Fine Art Photographic Library 60b; Fotomas Index 48t, 73c, 89br, 91; V.K. Guy 24; Robert Harding 8 (Roy Rainford), 69b, 85bl, 89tl (Adam Woolfit), 90t (Philip Craven); Historic Royal Palaces 58l & r, 59t; Angelo Hornak 59b; Jarrold Publishing 25b, 52, 63t, 68 (Neil Jinkerson), 84, 94; Leeds Castle 57t; Magdalene College, Oxford 44r; Marquess of Salisbury front cover l, 6, 41, 92; Marquess of Tavistock and Trustees of the Bedford Estate 49; Mary Evans 43r, 47b; Mary Rose Trust 17tr, 78cl; Museum of London 57b; National Maritime Museum 46/47; National Portrait Gallery front cover r, 9l & r, 10r, 13bl, 20b, 21t & b, 29l & r, 34l, 35, 39r, 40b, 77t, 89tr (detail); The National Trust 54b, 64 (Roy Twigge); Pepys Library, Magdalene College, Cambridge 17b; Private Collection 62; Public Record Office 13br, 23b; The Royal Collection 4/5, 14/15, 16/17, 28b, 38; From the RSC Collection with the permission of the Governors of the Royal Shakespeare Theatre 90bl; Shakespeare Birthplace Trust 76, 90br; Shakespeare's Globe 82 (Donald Cooper); Trinity College Library, Cambridge 56; V&A Picture Library 37l, 48b, 60t, 63b; Viscount de l'Ile 42; Woodmansterne 18t.

A CIP catalogue for this book is available from the British Library.

Published by:
Jarrold Publishing
Healey House, Dene Road, Andover, Hampshire, SP10 2AA
www.britguides.com

Set in Minion.
Printed in Singapore.

ISBN 13: 978 1 84165 126 2
ISBN 10: 1 84165 126 5   2/06

 Pitkin is an imprint of Jarrold Publishing, Norwich.

Autocratic, egotistical, sometimes visionary, they controlled the state with ruthless efficiency, re-establishing the governing authority at home that had been lost during the long-running Wars of the Roses, and at the same time gaining the respect of other European nations.

The Reformation, which presented a radical challenge to the authority of the Roman Catholic Church, was already swirling around Europe. In Tudor times, this revolutionary movement came to England. Catholics and Protestants fought for men's souls with a ferocious intensity that reached fanatical proportions in the middle of the 16th century. It was an upheaval of far-reaching political and social significance.

'There must be a beginning of any great matter, but the continuing unto the end until it be thoroughly finished yields the true glory.'

Francis Drake

SOLE

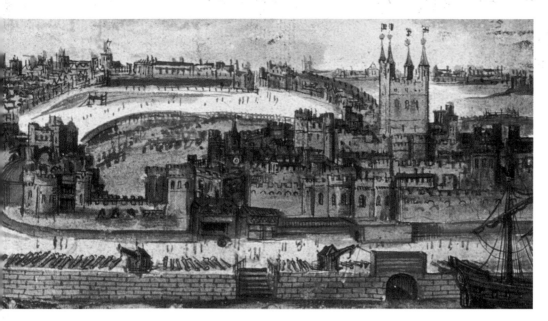

The Tudor age was an era of enterprise and opportunity, a time when men of modest means and humble background could achieve greatness and glory. There existed a mixture of avarice and idealism, of ostentation and sacrifice, as the newly rich flaunted their wealth while martyrs died selflessly for their cause. Bold explorers broadened the horizon of the known world. Some achieved fame and fortune, others perished unrewarded in far-flung corners of the globe.

During the Tudor era the nation's population doubled – towns grew enormously and London became the largest city in Europe. Immigrants arrived in droves. By the 1580s, one third of the population of Norwich were Flemish refugees escaping religious persecution in the Netherlands. They introduced new skills at a time when industry and commerce were becoming welcome alternatives to agriculture as

THE RAINBOW PORTRAIT
This classic portrait of Queen Elizabeth I was painted by Marcus Gheeraerts and is to be found at Hatfield House, once the home of her all-powerful minister, Sir Robert Cecil.

providers of wealth and employment. The Renaissance finally reached English shores. The kingdom established a growing international reputation for scholarship and literature, whilst producing William Shakespeare, the finest playwright the world has ever known.

Although peace reigned throughout the kingdom during the 16th century, apart from inconsequential minor rebellions, England remained in constant peril of invasion from its powerful Continental neighbours, France and Spain. Towards the end of the century, as the Spanish Armada sailed up the English Channel, the nation faced its greatest external threat since the Norman Conquest. England's famous victory over Spain represented the Tudors' finest military achievement, with far-reaching political consequences that brought the nation to the brink of greatness. England had come a long way since Henry Tudor arrived in 1485 to find a divided and dispirited nation. Just over one hundred years later the Tudors had fulfilled their destiny.

FAREWELL TO ARMS
By the end of the 16th century the musket had replaced the longbow as the foot soldier's main weapon in combat. This Tudor gentleman-at-arms carries a matchlock musket.

7

Hever Castle in Kent was owned by the Boleyn family and was the childhood home of Anne Boleyn. Henry VIII courted Anne on many occasions at Hever before she became his second wife.

THREE SUCCESSIVE TUDOR kings ruled England: the first of them, perhaps the shrewdest businessman ever to sit on the English throne; the second, a rumbustious showman; and the third, a religious fanatic who died before reaching manhood.

The throne had changed hands repeatedly during the Wars of the Roses (1455–85). During this period of civil war, two royal lines, the House of Lancaster and the House of York, both descended from King Edward III, fought over the English Crown. The nation was in chaos. A powerful man was needed to rule with authority and restore order – that man was Henry VII. When his handsome second son succeeded him as Henry VIII in 1509, England was a stable kingdom with its revenues fully restored. Henry VIII went to desperate lengths to ensure that his Crown passed to a son, and it did, although the young Edward VI reigned only for a short time.

The Tudors had acquired their kingdom by force of arms and were determined to keep it. Any insurgents, together with any individuals perceived to be a threat to the monarch, were speedily crushed and summarily executed: the Tudor kings did not merely reign – they ruled with a rod of iron. At the same time, they elevated the importance of the monarchy to new heights and greatly extended royal power. After Henry VIII had ascended the throne, the Tudor Court became a glittering showpiece, its magnificence the wonder of all Europe.

THE FIRST TUDOR KING
This portrait of Henry VII in the National Portrait Gallery in London is said to be the first Renaissance portrait to be painted in England.

HENRY VIII AGED 45
This portrait was painted the year that Henry married Jane Seymour. Although magnificently dressed, the king is ageing and overweight.

'His Majesty is the handsomest potentate I have ever set eyes on.'
Piero Pasqualigo, the Venetian envoy, about Henry VIII

9

HENRY VII, SUPREME ADMINISTRATOR

'Sad, serious and full of thoughts.'

A History of Henry VII,
Francis Bacon

THE WELSHMAN HENRY TUDOR was an extraordinary man. He had no experience of combat or military command, yet his small, heavily outnumbered army won one of the most decisive battles in English history, thereby giving him the Crown. His mother was a teenage widow when he was born at Pembroke Castle in the winter of 1457. Until 1485 he spent most of his adult life in Brittany, seeking refuge from the Wars of the Roses, and he had a better understanding of French than of English. Although he had received no training, Henry had an instinctive grasp of the qualities needed to be a successful king.

Henry was tall with fair hair and piercing blue eyes. Both shrewd and decisive, he inspired confidence, possessing a natural flair for choosing able men, invariably from humble backgrounds as he distrusted the aristocracy. Through his mother, Henry was a direct descendant of John of Gaunt, Duke of Lancaster, who was a son of Edward III and the father of the first Lancastrian king, Henry IV. The Crown had been in Yorkist hands since 1471, but Henry Tudor was now undisputed head of the House of Lancaster and he knew that kingdoms could be captured in combat.

Shortly after his coronation, Henry married his cousin Elizabeth, daughter of Edward IV and head of the House of York, thereby uniting the rival factions that had fought for so long. Elizabeth was tall and slender. Initially a political match, it became a happy marriage and when Elizabeth died in childbirth in 1503 Henry was devastated. He became a virtual recluse, his Court a dull place.

A TUDOR HARD MAN

Henry VII by the Italian sculptor Pietro Torrigiano. Henry was courteous, calculating, resolute and utterly ruthless, capturing the throne of England by force in the space of an afternoon.

HENRY'S BRIDE

Elizabeth of York was the daughter of Edward IV. Her marriage to Henry VII joined the houses of York and Lancaster, whose rival claims to the English throne had caused and prolonged the Wars of the Roses.

Henry was pious and industrious, yet avaricious and obsessed with money. A visiting Spaniard observed that he was happiest 'writing the accounts of his expenses in his own hand'. Henry ruled for nearly 24 years. In that time he restored the authority of the Crown and re-established law, order and a successful economy. Abroad he succeeded through ambassadors rather than with conquering armies, astutely strengthening political alliances by marrying his eldest son, Arthur, to Catherine of Aragon and his daughter, Margaret, to James IV of Scotland. Two successive pretenders, Lambert Simnel and Perkin Warbeck, unsuccessfully attempted a Yorkist come-back. The former was put to work in the royal kitchens, the latter executed.

Henry died in bed at Richmond Palace aged 52, leaving to his son a kingdom that was peaceful, prosperous and respected throughout Europe.

A DECISIVE ENCOUNTER
Henry's army, consisting largely of foreign mercenaries, defeated Richard III's forces close to the small Leicestershire town of Market Bosworth in 1485. Here, on Bosworth Field, Lord Stanley is seen putting Richard's crown onto Henry's head.

THE BATTLE OF BOSWORTH

The Italian Polydore Vergil wrote about Richard III's last battle, recording that the king might have got away: **'for they that were about him, seeing the soldiers even from the first stroke to lift up their weapons feebly and faintly, and some of them to depart the field secretly, suspected treason and exhorted him to flee.'** Richard rejected the offer of swift horses and 'came to the fight with the crown upon his head' – whence it was later taken to be placed on the brow of the victor, Henry Tudor. Richard was the last English king to be killed in battle.

HENRY AS A YOUNG MAN

The good looks and fine bearing of the youthful King Henry led one admiring ambassador to describe him as 'the most handsomest potentate'. Painted by an unknown artist, this picture hangs in the National Portrait Gallery, London.

WHEN HENRY VII DIED in April 1509, the new king, just 18 years old, lost no time in making changes. During the last years of his father's life Prince Henry had lived in virtual isolation, so afraid had his father been that he might catch the dreaded 'sweating sickness', a highly infectious fever that could kill within hours.

Almost immediately after his father's death, Henry married Catherine of Aragon, his brother's widow, and together they brought gaiety and spectacular entertainment back into Court life. Henry spent his days hunting, hawking, shooting with a bow or a gun and, when not out hunting, he played musical instruments, sang and danced. He was energetic and charismatic.

Unlike his father, the young King Henry displayed little enthusiasm for the affairs of state, preferring to leave these tasks to those he appointed: the glory and immortality he was looking for lay in war. A hundred years earlier, Henry V had won the Battle of Agincourt, conquered Normandy and become heir to the French Crown, although he died too soon to succeed to the French throne. Henry VIII wanted to achieve as much and more, and he was determined to lead his army into battle himself. He loved jousting and every day he practised in the tiltyards. In the first years of his reign he relied on his father's ministers for advice, but, although they advised against war, he became increasingly eager to prove himself on the battlefield.

Henry's happiness seemed complete when, on New Year's Day in 1511, his wife Catherine gave birth to a son, who was christened Henry. The feasting and tournament to celebrate went on for weeks, but, unhappily, the baby lived for less than two months. To assuage his disappointment, Henry threw himself into preparing for war.

Henry's army captured a couple of minor towns in Normandy and vanquished a French army at the Battle of the Spurs, so-called on account of the speed at which the French force fled the field. Meanwhile, in Henry's absence, a Scottish army had invaded England but were

> *'Our king does not desire gold or gems or precious metals, but virtue, glory, immortality.'*
>
> Lord Mountjoy, writing of Henry VIII to the scholar Erasmus in 1509

HENRY VIII'S FIRST WIFE

Catherine of Aragon, daughter of the king of Spain, became the first of Henry's six wives. Catherine had previously been married to Henry's elder brother Arthur, who died aged 16, but claimed that her earlier marriage was unconsummated.

heavily defeated in 1513 at the Battle of Flodden in Northumberland. The body of Scottish king James IV, husband of Henry's elder sister Margaret, was discovered under one of the large piles of corpses that littered the battlefield.

These victories brought Henry considerable prestige but at enormous cost, since the campaigns used up all the money so carefully accumulated by Henry VII. However, the English king was now a force to be reckoned with by political heavyweights such as Charles V, Emperor of the Holy Roman Empire, and François I of France. Henry VIII had truly arrived as a player on the international stage and, according to the perceptive Italian statesman Niccolò Machiavelli, was 'rich, ferocious, and greedy for glory'.

A CELEBRATION JOUST

To celebrate the birth of a son in 1511, Henry organized a grand tournament at which the king was the star performer. Sadly, his much-wanted son and heir died shortly afterwards.

THE GOLDEN BULL MEDAL

This gold medal was presented to King Henry VIII by Pope Clement VII, confirming the king as 'Defender of the Faith'. Despite his break with Rome, Henry retained this title and the letters 'F D' still appear on British coins.

THE FIELD OF CLOTH OF GOLD

FULL METAL JACKET

A suit of armour made for Henry by his armoury workshop at Greenwich in 1515. Henry's horse was also well protected.

HENRY'S STANDING IN EUROPE was reflected by the extravagance of the diplomatic meeting known as the Field of Cloth of Gold in the early summer of 1520. Intended as a serious Anglo-French summit meeting, this epic encounter proved to be a spectacular exercise in royal one-upmanship as the two monarchs strove to outdo each other in regal splendour, regardless of cost. Henry spent over £4 million, then a huge sum, while the expenditure of French king François I took more than a decade to repay.

Henry met François outside Calais, the last remaining English territory in France. Accompanied by Queen Catherine, Cardinal Wolsey and some 4,000 retainers, Henry constructed a vast temporary palace, complete with battlements and gatehouse. Outside, jets of claret, spiced wine and

AN EXTRAVAGANT DISPLAY OF ONE-UPMANSHIP

Onlookers were amazed at the sheer magnificence of this grand encounter between Henry and the French king, François I.

water gushed from a gilded fountain. François riposted by erecting over 400 giant tents, fashioned in gold brocade, glittering in the warm June sunshine. Thus it was that the event became known as the Field of Cloth of Gold.

~

There followed two weeks of feasting, jousting tournaments and dancing late into the night. The two monarchs met each other daily, wearing progressively more extravagant outfits, yet whilst there was plenty of elaborate ritual and flowery rhetoric, little of lasting significance was achieved in this costly encounter as neither monarch trusted the other. 'They hate each other cordially,' quipped a cynical Venetian observer. There was much posturing and preening but little meaningful political discussion. Two weeks later, Henry signed a treaty with François I's arch-enemy, Emperor Charles V, and within two years England was once more at war with France.

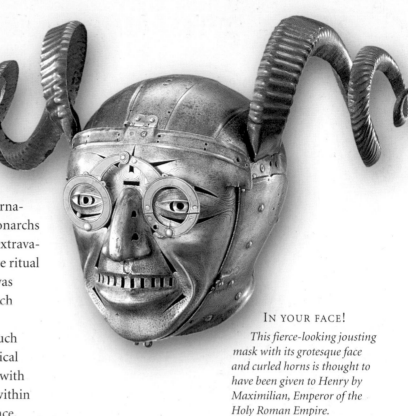

IN YOUR FACE!
This fierce-looking jousting mask with its grotesque face and curled horns is thought to have been given to Henry by Maximilian, Emperor of the Holy Roman Empire.

PRIDE GOETH BEFORE A FALL

'Come, you shall wrestle with me,' boomed Henry as he challenged François to a wrestling match, only to be hurled speedily and unexpectedly to the ground by the smaller French king. Henry scrambled to his feet, demanding a second round, but was foiled by the call to supper. Henry was deeply embarrassed. A French knight, the Sieur de Fleuranges, was present to record the event, but no English observer thought it prudent to report the royal fall. Henry's honour was partially restored, however, when he managed to defeat François at archery.

HENRY VIII's NAVY

TUDOR LIFE ON THE OCEAN WAVE

The English fleet at Dover in 1520, ready to transport Henry and Queen Catherine across the Channel to meet the French king. One of the escort ships was the Mary Rose, *named after Henry's favourite sister.*

THE DIPLOMATIC SUCCESSES of Henry VIII in Europe were backed up by an effective and modern navy. Although this navy had been founded by Henry VII, it was his son who turned it into a powerful fighting force. He inherited only five warships from his father, two of which were large, four-masted carracks, several storeys high.

In his own reign, Henry VIII built some 59 ships, large and small, bought another 26 vessels and captured a further 13.

Henry was fascinated both by ships and by guns and he was the first English ruler to build warships that carried heavy guns for sinking enemy ships. Previously, ships had

16

TUDOR CANNON

Some of the earliest cast-bronze guns made for Henry have been recovered along with the wreck of the Mary Rose. *The wreck, with cannon and other artefacts, is superbly displayed within Portsmouth Dockyard.*

been used in war to transport the army and, in sea battles, simply as platforms from which soldiers could board enemy ships to fight hand to hand. At sea trials in 1513, however, the *Mary Rose*, specially built to carry heavy guns, outsailed all the other ships.

Henry, annoyed that the king of Scotland had a larger ship than any of his, set his shipyards to work. In 1514 the huge and splendid *Great Harry* was launched. It carried 21 heavy guns and 700 men and on state occasions was decked out with sails made from cloth of gold.

During Henry's lifetime Spanish ships discovered the Americas and, under Ferdinand Magellan, sailed around the world, but Henry seldom looked beyond Europe. By the time he died in 1547, he had built up a navy of about 50 serviceable ships, capable of taking on the fleets of Spain, France or the Netherlands. The creation of a permanent English fleet was one of Henry's most significant achievements. It would evolve into the Royal Navy and become a powerful force to be used to protect trade and England's overseas colonies.

THE SINKING OF THE MARY ROSE

The sinking of the *Mary Rose* was the greatest English maritime disaster of the Tudor age. As she prepared to fight an invading French fleet off Portsmouth in 1545, the *Mary Rose* fired a broadside from her starboard guns and was beginning to change direction when disaster struck. A sudden strong gust of wind caused the ship to heel violently over and a torrent of water poured in through the open gun ports. The *Mary Rose* capsized and sank deep into the swirling waters of the Solent. Sir George Carew, Vice Admiral of the Fleet, Captain Roger Grenville and most of the 700 crew were drowned, their despairing cries heard by the horrified spectators on the shore.

THE GREAT HARRY

This mighty warship was part of Henry's massive programme of naval rearmament that was needed to counter powerful foreign fleets that threatened England's security.

HENRY'S SEARCH FOR A SON

'If a man takes his brother's wife, it is impurity; he has uncovered his brother's nakedness, they shall be childless.'

Leviticus 20, verse 21

BY 1526 HENRY KNEW that Catherine would never bear him the son he so badly wanted. After numerous pregnancies only a daughter, Mary, born in 1516, had survived, and Catherine's child-bearing years were clearly over. Why, Henry wondered, had God denied him a legitimate heir? He concluded that he had angered God by marrying Catherine, his brother's widow, an action that had been sanctioned by the Pope but was forbidden by the Bible.

❧

Then Henry fell passionately in love with Anne Boleyn, one of Catherine's ladies-in-waiting, and became convinced that only by marrying Anne could he get the son he longed for. He threw himself into what he called his 'Great Matter' – extracting himself from his marriage to Catherine. He decided that the special dispensation given by Pope Julius II that had allowed him to marry Catherine after Arthur's death was invalid and so was the marriage, but Catherine did not agree. Henry ordered Wolsey to secure an annulment

ANNE BOLEYN

Henry's second wife was a consummate manipulator who ultimately lost Henry's love when she failed to provide a healthy son and heir. 'I see that God does not mean me to have male children,' he muttered angrily to her.

CATHERINE ARGUES HER CASE

This Victorian painting shows an imperious Queen Catherine passionately presenting her case to King Henry and Cardinals Wolsey and Campeggio. Catherine refused to consider an annulment of her marriage with Henry.

of his marriage from the Pope. In 1529 the Pope set up a court conducted by Cardinals Wolsey and Campeggio to examine the case, but Campeggio, anxious not to upset Charles V of Spain, Catherine's nephew, made sure that a verdict was not reached.

Wolsey was stripped of the chancellorship and banished to York where he was charged with treason. En route to the Tower of London, Wolsey fell ill and died. In 1533 Henry finally lost patience with Catherine. Rejecting the Pope's authority, he obtained a decree of nullity from the new Archbishop of Canterbury, Thomas Cranmer. By that time Anne was pregnant. Henry was so certain that this time he would have a son that he had notices of the birth of the 'prince' prepared in advance. When a daughter, Elizabeth, was born on 7 September 1533, the notices were hastily changed to 'princess', but the celebrations were cancelled and Henry did not attend the christening.

When Anne's next two pregnancies ended in miscarriage, she knew that her position was perilous. Henry's second marriage was following the same course as his first and he now wanted rid of his queen. In April a royal commission found 'evidence' that Anne had committed adultery with five men, one of them her brother, and in May 1536 they were all executed. Henry did not mourn Anne's passing but turned his attention to his new love, Jane Seymour. They were betrothed the day after Anne's execution and married on 30 May 1536.

Now, Henry believed, he could start again with his 'most dear and most entirely beloved' wife. On 12 October 1537 Jane gave birth to a son, Edward, at Hampton Court. But Henry's joy was short-lived: Jane contracted childbed fever and died 11 days after giving birth. This time Henry was grief-stricken. He wore black and remained in mourning until February the following year.

Henry's third wife

Anne Boleyn was quickly replaced by Jane Seymour, who soon managed to give Henry the son he sought so obsessively. Sadly, she died shortly after his birth.

THE KING'S MEN

HENRY VIII RELIED heavily on the men he chose to run his affairs of state. Fortunately he possessed the ability to pick very capable men to do the job for him, yet regrettably he was quick to discard those who failed to carry out his wishes, disagreed with him or made him unpopular. First to go were his father's clever yet thoroughly disliked ministers, Richard Empson and Edmund Dudley, both summarily executed in the interest of expediency. They were replaced by Thomas Wolsey, a butcher's son from Ipswich, who had entered the Church.

Under Henry, Wolsey progressively became Lord Chancellor, Archbishop of York and a cardinal with ambitions to be Pope. Wolsey was the last of the great medieval-style churchmen to wield so much power in England, a man of enormous talent who did much to fulfil Henry's desire for centralized government, yet his arrogance, extravagance and ostentatious lifestyle upset the Tudor elite, who were envious of his powerful influence with the king. Wolsey's fall from power cleared the way for Henry to appoint new men, such as Cranmer and Cromwell, to carry out his bidding.

THE GOOD SERVANT WHO PUT GOD FIRST

Sir Thomas More was devoted to Henry, but in the end 'the King's good servant' obeyed his conscience and not his earthly master. More was duly executed at the Tower of London.

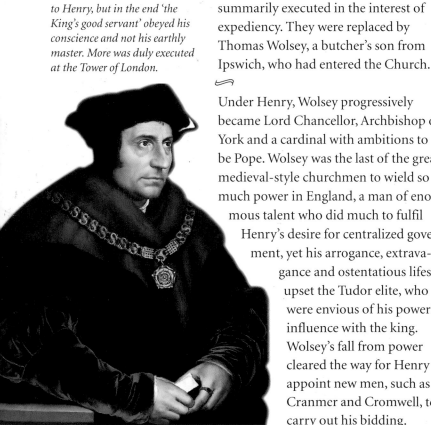

KING AND CARDINAL

Thomas Wolsey rose from humble beginnings to become the king's most trusted and astute advisor. His rise to success was swift, his demise was equally so, following his failure to secure Henry's divorce from Catherine.

Thomas Cranmer was chaplain to the Boleyn family so when Henry wooed Anne Boleyn Cranmer came into contact with the king. He ingeniously suggested that all the major European universities should be consulted in the matter of the king's divorce. Their favourable response led to Cranmer becoming Ambassador to

PROTESTANT FIREBRAND

Thomas Cranmer, a leading Protestant intellectual, was appointed Archbishop of Canterbury in 1533. The previous year he had secretly married the niece of a German Protestant reformer.

the Holy Roman Empire and after that Archbishop of Canterbury. The fervently Protestant Cranmer encouraged Henry with the Act of Supremacy in 1534, by which the king replaced the Pope as the head of the Church in England.

Thomas More, a leading intellectual and close friend of the Dutch scholar Erasmus, followed Wolsey as Lord Chancellor. A man of conscience and strong spiritual beliefs, More refused to approve of the king's divorce or accept him as head of the Church in England. More was duly consigned to the Tower of London on a charge of treason and, in spite of a skilful defence at his trial, was condemned to death and executed in July 1535. Henry was excommunicated by the Pope while Thomas More was later created a saint.

The next Lord Chancellor was Thomas Cromwell, a blacksmith's son who became a lawyer and worked under Wolsey. Cromwell was highly intelligent and hugely energetic, ruthless and ambitious, yet without the self-aggrandizement of Wolsey. He is remembered by many as the man who persuaded Henry to execute Anne Boleyn and dissolve the monasteries. Yet, in his ten years of office, Cromwell totally reformed the administration of the State and effectively set the agenda for future government procedures. His biggest mistake was arranging the king's marriage to Anne of Cleves (see page 28). Cromwell was despatched to the Tower and beheaded in 1540.

MORE'S SUCCESSOR

Thomas Cromwell, a grammar-school boy made good, worked for Wolsey for a time, then profited from the Cardinal's disgrace and More's fatal defiance of the king.

SURRENDER OF THE PIOUS

A Victorian painting depicts King Henry's commissioners taking over Syon Nunnery, one of the few religious houses whose inhabitants had continued to live a strict and pious life.

THE REFORMATION BEGAN in Europe in 1517 when Martin Luther, a German monk, nailed his 95 Theses, protesting against abuses in the Church, to a church door in Wittenberg, Germany. The movement rapidly spread across Europe and by 1550 Protestantism was established across almost half of the Continent. Henry VIII was well aware of the rising tide of Protestantism and at first thoroughly disapproved of it. In 1521 the Pope granted him the title 'Fidei Defensor' (Defender of the Faith) for his book *The Defence of the Seven Sacraments*, in which Henry defended the Roman Catholic Church against Luther's attacks.

When the Pope declined to grant him a divorce, however, Henry became increasingly defiant until finally, under the Act of Supremacy passed by Parliament in 1534, he pronounced himself head of the Church in England. Although the Act gave statutory recognition to the Reformation in England, Henry continued to think of himself as a true Catholic. In opposing Rome, his motives were personal and material, rather than religious. Likewise the ensuing dissolution of the monasteries can be seen as an asset-stripping exercise to aid the state coffers rather than a desire on Henry's part to confront Roman Catholicism.

But, as elsewhere in the continent of Europe, the Reformation brought strife to England. Initially many people were pleased to be free of the papacy, but when Sir Thomas More and Bishop John Fisher were executed for refusing to take the oath demanded by the Act of Supremacy, the mood changed. Many ordinary people then lived in fear as, all over the country, hundreds of 'loyal citizens' rushed to accuse their neighbours, friends and relatives of continuing loyalty to Rome – now an act of treason.

At first, too, there was popular support for the dissolution of the monasteries. In 1535 Henry ordered his minister Thomas Cromwell to investigate the monasteries' estates and holy practices. Although the commissioners found some monasteries run by hard-working and dedicated monks or nuns, most reports told of decaying buildings and corrupt clergy, some of whom were found with prostitutes in their religious houses. In spring 1536 Parliament agreed to dissolve the 300 smallest monasteries. The larger monasteries followed soon after. The monks and nuns were given pensions and the monasteries' valuable treasures were removed. The walls were torn down and the stained glass smashed by Henry's men, while ordinary people often joined in the looting.

The changes happened so quickly that many people became uneasy and some began to protest. In the north of England the protest culminated in a popular uprising known as the Pilgrimage of Grace. Determined that his authority should not be questioned, Henry ordered that the rebels be treated without mercy. Instead of being the much-loved king of earlier years, Henry was now feared and hated by his people.

HENRY AT PRAYER

This picture comes from the Black Book of the Garter. *Henry was indeed a pious man yet never hesitated to use religion to further his own purposes.*

CHURCH VALUATION

This illuminated document details all the Church's estates together with their treasures. One of Henry's primary motives in dissolving the monasteries was to seize their prodigious wealth for his own use.

MONASTERIES IN RUINS

THE DISSOLUTION OF THE monasteries was an acutely traumatic time for their inhabitants whose well-ordered lives had altered little for centuries. Many monastic communities had indeed become corrupt and run down. The numbers of monks and nuns had declined relentlessly, as fewer people experienced the spiritual desire or the material need to seek monastic sanctuary. Nevertheless the monasteries provided a living for lay people, particularly in remote communities where there was little prospect of alternative employment. They also provided vital medical facilities for the sick. Suddenly, throughout England, from Fountains Abbey in Yorkshire, hitherto the largest monastery in the country, down to St Augustine's in Kent, everything was to change for ever.

ﻌ

The fate of Hailes Abbey in Gloucestershire was sealed when King Henry's commissioners discovered that this Cistercian community's so-called phial of Holy Blood, which made their abbey one of the nation's major pilgrimage attractions, was actually an outrageous fake. One year later, on Christmas Eve 1539, Hailes was closed. Abbot Sagar and

FOUNTAINS ABBEY

The ruins of this huge Cistercian abbey on the banks of the River Skell in Yorkshire are almost as they were left by Henry's men more than 450 years ago.

21 monks were given pensions and Cromwell informed that 'right honest sorts of jewels' plate, ornaments and money we do safely reserve unto the King's Highnes use'. Three years later the Crown sold Hailes to Richard Andrews, a large-scale dealer in monastic property, and its long decline into ruin began.

Today the ruins of Hailes can be seen amidst the woods and meadows of the Northern Cotswolds, a few miles north-east of Cheltenham. A range of arches around the cloister, part of the north end of the refectory, together with walls worn down almost to foundation level, are all that remain of a monastery founded in the mid-13th century.

PROPERTY CONVERSION

Saint Augustine's Abbey, Canterbury, was dissolved and destroyed in 1538, leaving only ruined stone columns and arches. Henry rebuilt it using brick to construct yet another royal palace.

HAILES ABBEY

This abbey was founded by Richard, Earl of Cornwall, in gratitude for surviving a savage storm at sea when returning from the Crusades in October 1242. It is now owned by The National Trust.

DEATH FOR AN ABBOT

Richard Whiting had reluctantly been elected Abbot of Glastonbury Abbey in Somerset in February 1525, **'an upright and religious monk and a priest commendable for his life, virtues and learning,'** according to an approving Cardinal Wolsey. The abbot had consented to Henry's divorce from Catherine of Aragon, together with the break with Rome, and did not oppose the dissolution of his monastery. However, he had unwittingly antagonized Thomas Cromwell, who condemned him as a traitor. On 15 November 1539 the frail, elderly abbot was bound to a sheep's hurdle and dragged to the summit of Glastonbury Tor. There he was hanged and his corpse hacked into four pieces. It was one of the worst atrocities of Henry's progressively more brutal reign.

MILITARY POWER

'Let slip the dogs of war.'

Tamburlaine,
Christopher Marlowe

As Henry VIII's reign continued he became more and more preoccupied with the safety of his kingdom. The break with Rome had antagonized the powerful Roman Catholic countries of Continental Europe. Henry was particularly alarmed by the Treaty of Toledo in 1539, when the erstwhile enemies Charles V, Emperor of the Holy Roman Empire, and the French king, François I, joined forces. The English monarch immediately began preparations to resist invasion by strengthening his defences all along the south coast from Deal in Kent to St Mawes in West Cornwall.

This was the nation's largest fortress-building programme since the 14th century, using all available building material including that from the former monasteries. Henry personally supervised the construction of these massive new fortifications – the latest in military technology. The series of forts and castles provided a platform for an impressive range of firepower – the bastions at Deal, designed and built by Henry, contained 119 cannon. The cloverleaf pattern of the defences here represent the latest military thinking, the circular walls providing the maximum field of fire whilst deflecting incoming cannon balls. Henry paid particular attention to constructing elaborate defences at his major ports. Southsea, which protected the entrance to Portsmouth harbour, was considered to be the most sophisticated of his fortifications. It was from the battlements here that the king

KING OF THE CASTLE
Henry's castle at Deal was built in 1540 and garrisoned by only 25 men. Its guns could fire red-hot cannon balls more than 3 kilometres (1.5 miles).

A CORNISH CASTLE
Henry built St Mawes Castle in conjunction with the fortress at Pendennis on the other side of the estuary in order to protect the large, safe anchorage at Falmouth.

However, all Henry's military activity inevitably cost large sums of money. 'What infinite sums of money the king's grace hath spent already invading France … at this hour hath not one foot of land more in France than his most noble father had,' complained Archbishop Warham during the first half of Henry's reign. So it continued: little glory and yet great expense. Most of the financial resources he had inherited from his father, together with much of the proceeds from the dissolution of the monasteries, was spent in pursuit of vain ambitions in France.

was watching the English fleet engaging with French ships in 1545, when to his horror the *Mary Rose* suddenly capsized and sank (see page 17).

Henry had long held ambitions for reconquering France, but he was no Henry V, nor was there to be another Agincourt. In spite of numerous excursions, often with the king leading his troops, there was little to show for their efforts, apart from the temporary capture of Boulogne in 1544. His major military achievement was the establishment of a formidable and permanent English navy, well respected by major continental foreign powers, which conceivably reduced the threat of invasion. Likewise, his enthusiasm for new weapon technology and state-of-the-art fortifications heralded the end of the longbow and the old-style medieval castle. His encouragement of a gun-founding industry did much to improve the nation's artillery both on land and at sea.

THE SIEGE OF BOULOGNE
Henry was in high spirits when Boulogne surrendered after a three-month siege. It was a temporary triumph, however, as the French soon recaptured it.

HIDDEN GUNS
Gunmakers have sometimes skilfully incorporated guns into other weapons. There are three gun barrels concealed in the head of the mace on the right and there is a single barrel in the boss of the shield. Both of these ingenious pieces belonged to Henry VIII.

'His conscience has crept too near to another lady.'

Henry VIII, *William Shakespeare*

As HENRY PURSUED MILITARY means to counter threats from France and Spain, his Lord Chancellor, Thomas Cromwell, sought diplomatic means, using the lure of a marriage with Henry, now one of Europe's powerful leaders. Several women were suggested, including the daughter of French king François I. At one point, Henry even suggested that all the eligible women in France should be brought to Calais for him to inspect, but the French ambassador was outraged: if the ladies were to be paraded like ponies, 'maybe your Grace would like to mount them one after another, and keep the one you find to be the best broken in?'

Then Cromwell suggested that an alliance with the Protestant Duchy of Cleves would strengthen his position against France and Spain. The Duke, who was leader of the Protestants of western Germany, had two unmarried sisters. Henry was interested, but insisted on seeing a portrait before committing himself. Holbein travelled to Cleves and painted the two sisters. Henry was satisfied. A marriage contract was drawn up between himself and Anne of Cleves, but as soon as Henry met her he knew he had made a mistake. The wedding went ahead in January 1540, but six months later Henry was divorced.

Henry's next marriage was an even greater disaster. He fell in love with Catherine Howard, a vivacious young girl of 19 who had just come to Court and who, Henry was certain, would rejuvenate him. Henry adored Catherine

ANNE OF CLEVES

Holbein's portrait was said to be a good likeness of Anne, yet when Henry first saw her he said that she looked like his horse and nicknamed her the 'Flanders mare'.

CATHERINE HOWARD

The sexy but foolish niece of the Duke of Norfolk was a pretty pawn in the Duke's deadly game to bring down Thomas Cromwell.

and gave her lavish gifts, including land and houses. He was all the more wounded and enraged when in December 1541 he was presented with proof that she was unfaithful to him. Henry showed Catherine no mercy: her lovers, Thomas Culpepper and Francis Dereham, were both executed in December and Catherine herself was beheaded on 13 February 1542.

In 1543 he married his sixth wife, Catherine Parr, and with her he found not the heady excitement that Anne Boleyn and Catherine Howard had inspired, but rather contentment and companionship. Henry's new wife calmed him when he was angry and comforted him when he was ill or depressed. Henry, by now grossly overweight and in constant pain from a badly ulcerated leg, became progressively more bad tempered and feared. He spent much time alone, sending Catherine and most of the Court to Greenwich for Christmas 1546, while he remained at Whitehall. Suddenly the following month

Henry summoned Archbishop Cranmer, and in the early hours of 28 January 1547 he died, happy in the knowledge that he had a son to inherit his kingdom.

DEATH OF A KING

This allegorical painting by an unknown artist shows Henry on his deathbed pointing symbolically towards his son Edward as his successor.

HENRY'S SIXTH AND FINAL WIFE

Catherine Parr had already been widowed twice when Henry proposed to her in 1543. Not the prettiest but certainly the cleverest of his wives, Catherine provided Henry with solace in his declining years.

FATHER AND SON

This Victorian picture shows a happy King Henry playing with young Prince Edward in the royal nursery at Hampton Court Palace.

WHEN EDWARD WAS BORN at Hampton Court in the autumn of 1537, the king wept tears of joy and the Royal Court was in rapture. After 28 years on the throne Henry had at last produced the long-awaited son and heir. 'We all hungered after a prince so long that there was as much rejoicing as at the birth of John the Baptist,' declared Bishop Hugh Latimer.

Mindful of his son's health, Henry sent him to live in the country, so Edward, who had lost his mother shortly after his birth, was also deprived of a father during his formative years. At an early age the young prince commenced a classical education in such subjects as Latin, Greek and philosophy, from a trio of Cambridge scholars, John Cheke, William Grindal and Roger Ascham. All of these eminent men were devoted to the emerging Protestant creed, and conceivably this was when Edward began to acquire his enthusiasm for 'the new faith'.

After his father had married his sixth wife in 1543, Edward spent more time at Court and soon began to adopt his father's mannerisms. William Scrots' striking portrait, now in the Royal Collection,

depicts a thin, pale-faced prince, manfully attempting Henry's arrogant stance. When Henry died in 1547, Edward was only nine years of age. He succeeded as king with his strongly Protestant uncle, Edward Seymour, soon to be Duke of Somerset, as Regent and Lord Protector. Seymour, however, quickly became unpopular, both for his incompetence in ruling the country and for his imposition of Protestantism. In 1549 he was deposed by the Earl of Warwick and sent to the Tower of London to be executed as a traitor.

The precocious young king was clever yet callous, seemingly indifferent to the fate of the victims of the constant power struggles that were such a feature of the Tudor era, including both his uncles, Edward and Thomas Seymour. Under the influence of Archbishop Cranmer, Edward zealously pursued religious reform throughout his kingdom. In the churches statues were destroyed, wall paintings whitewashed and stained-glass windows smashed in an

orgy of iconoclasm, that saw the ritual of old-style Roman Catholicism give way to a hard-line Protestantism.

Had Edward lived longer, he might have become an extremist, authoritarian despot, but he was a delicate youth and contracted what is believed to have been tuberculosis. 'Lord God free me from this calumnious life,' was Edward's anguished cry on his deathbed at Greenwich in the summer of 1553. He was 15. The last of the Tudor kings had been on the throne barely six years.

A PRINCE IN PROFILE

Prince Edward as a boy, one of many portraits the king commissioned of his son, who had the same reddish hair as his father and his half-sister Elizabeth.

ELIZABETHAN CONNECTIONS

The old palace at Hatfield in Hertfordshire featured prominently in the life of Queen Elizabeth: she was at Hatfield when she first learned she had become queen and, shortly after acquiring the throne, she held her first Privy Council meeting here.

PROCESSION OF THE KNIGHTS OF THE GARTER

These coloured engravings of 1576 show Queen Elizabeth at the rear of the annual procession of Knights of the Garter on St George's Day at Windsor. By 1595 the occasion had become so popular the procession made its way three times around the courtyard.

HISTORY WAS MADE IN the summer of 1553 when Mary became the first woman to succeed to the English throne. In turn she was followed by Elizabeth. Mary's reign was beset by strife, yet it was mercifully short; Elizabeth's was conceivably the most glorious in the nation's history.

As monarchs, the Tudor queens had to establish the principle that a woman could take personal charge of the country. In Tudor England the perceived wisdom was that a queen would always be subordinate to her husband. Both Mary and Elizabeth were single when they came to the throne: Mary made the mistake of marrying a Catholic foreigner, whilst Elizabeth side-stepped the problem by staying single throughout her life, a Virgin Queen, 'already bound to a husband which is the Kingdom of England,' as she famously declared. For all her faults, Mary pioneered the concept of a female monarch, accustoming the kingdom to feminine rule. Elizabeth used her sex to maximum advantage, to charm, cajole and manipulate the men around her. She could also display a steely resolve equal to that of any man. 'I know I have the body of a weak and feeble woman but I have the heart and stomach of a king and of a king of England too,' declaimed Elizabeth, astride a magnificent white charger, reviewing her troops as her kingdom was threatened by the Spanish Armada.

TUDOR QUEENS

Mary being welcomed to London in 1553, just after she became queen following the death of her half-brother Edward VI. Behind her is Princess Elizabeth, who would succeed her in 1558.

QUEEN MARY I

THE STAUNCHLY ROMAN CATHOLIC Mary was among the most reviled, unhappy and unsuccessful of English monarchs. As a child, when her father tired of her mother Catherine of Aragon, she was banished from the Court and declared illegitimate. For many years Mary lived a lonely life in humble surroundings, separated from her mother and publicly humiliated by Anne Boleyn. She was eventually allowed to return to Court only after being persuaded to acknowledge her father's divorce from her mother and his authority as head of the English Church. Mary then had to watch as her half-brother Edward, ruthlessly pressed the cause of Protestantism across the nation.

When Edward died in 1553, Mary rallied her supporters to quash the attempt to establish her niece, the Protestant Lady Jane Grey, as queen. By that time Mary was 37 years old, small and rather dowdy: 'a perfect saint who dresses badly,' sneered an observer. Contemporary portraits depict a woman with a short-sighted stare and a small, thin-lipped mouth. She had a hoarse, rather masculine voice and was really rather shy.

Mary was also exceedingly dogmatic, possessing the obstinacy of other Tudor monarchs but without their common sense; she berated her Privy Councillors and ignored their advice, particularly in

UNHAPPY PRINCESS

Princess Mary was separated from her mother in 1532 and never saw her again. Mary was declared illegitimate and banned from Court for several years.

QUEEN FOR NINE DAYS

Paul Delaroche's melodramatic picture shows the execution of Lady Jane Grey. In reality, the unfortunate Jane was beheaded out of doors on Tower Green. Edward VI had wanted her to succeed him to maintain the Protestant succession.

'The most unhappy lady in Christendom.'

Mary's observation about herself

the all-important choice of a husband. Half Spanish herself, Mary's marriage to Prince Philip of Spain, ten years her junior, not long after she became queen, was the start of her unpopularity. Her citizens had no wish to see this Catholic foreigner sharing her throne or her bed.

It was Mary's fanatical determination, however, to turn the religious clock back and restore Roman Catholicism that proved her undoing. Those who opposed her were condemned as heretics and burned at the stake. The now frail and aged Archbishop Cramner, together with numerous ordinary people, died in agony. The flames that consumed them also destroyed the support of her people. Meanwhile Philip became King of Spain and returned to his native land.

Mary had lost the affection of her husband and of her citizens; soon she was to lose her life. She developed what is thought to have been ovarian cancer, which had probably also killed her mother, and died in the night of 17 November 1558, having reluctantly acknowledged her Protestant half-sister Elizabeth as her successor.

THE SPANISH SUITOR

Philip had married Mary before he became King of Spain. When Mary died he supported the succession of Elizabeth to the English throne and promptly proposed marriage to her.

35

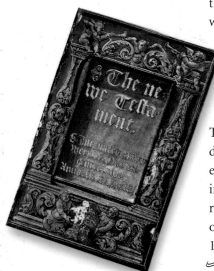

THE FIRST ENGLISH BIBLE

In 1534 William Tyndale translated and published the New Testament in English for the first time. Today, copies are to be found in the library of St Paul's Cathedral and in the British Library, London.

ONE OF THE MOST fundamental changes that occurred in 16th-century England was the replacement of traditional Catholicism by Protestantism, which began when Henry VIII superseded the Pope as head of the Church of England in 1534. The king commanded that Bibles recently translated by William Tyndale and Miles Coverdale should be displayed throughout his kingdom, giving everyone the chance to read the scriptures in English for the first time. English also replaced Latin in church services. Closure of the monasteries five years later removed 10,000 Catholic monks.

Edward VI and the protectors who ruled in his name accelerated the move into Protestantism. Archbishop Cranmer's Prayer Book was introduced throughout the nation, but it was opposed by Roman Catholics and Protestants alike, since it fudged the central issue of the mass. Were the consecrated bread and wine miraculously changed into the body and blood of Christ, or was the sacrament simply a commemoration of Christ? For Mary, who restored Catholicism as soon as she became ruler, there was no doubt that the former was true. Those who opposed her were burned at the stake. Thousands of ordinary people died, creating lasting bitterness and anti-Catholic prejudice.

Elizabeth inherited a demoralized and confused kingdom, yet by the end of her reign the Church in England was firmly Protestant. The queen achieved this largely through moderation and tolerance. William Byrd, her organist at the Chapel

'A very sharp maintainer of the purer religion.'

William Camden describing the fervent Protestant Sir Francis Walsingham

BURNED AT THE STAKE

In the autumn of 1555, two prominent Protestant bishops, Hugh Latimer and Nicholas Ridley, were tied to stakes on top of a large pile of faggots in Broad Street outside Balliol College, Oxford. Both men had been condemned to death for heresy, having publicly preached against Roman Catholicism. **'Be of good comfort Master Ridley, and play the man. We shall this day light such a candle by God's grace in England, as I trust shall never be put out,'** shouted Latimer as flames engulfed them and a sickening smell of burning flesh filled the air. The fire was so fierce that the doors of the entrance to Balliol were badly scorched. Today, an iron cross in the road marks the scene of their martyrdom.

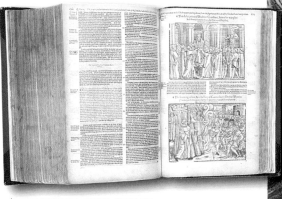

A RELIGIOUS BEST-SELLER

Foxe's Book of Martyrs, *first published in 1563, did much to popularize Protestantism and stir up antagonism towards Catholicism during Elizabeth's time. It ran to seven editions during her reign.*

QUEEN ELIZABETH AT PRAYER

Elizabeth was a devout, yet not overly fanatical, Protestant. Unlike Mary, she did not seek to impose religion on her subjects – 'not wishing to open windows into men's souls', according to Francis Bacon.

Royal, was Catholic, as was Lord Howard of Effingham, commander of the English Fleet, and other prominent members of the Court. However, change was not accomplished without a theological tussle. Puritan extremists considered religious reform was insufficient. Perceived popish ornaments in churches were destroyed and exquisite medieval craftsmanship smashed by religious zealots. Some Jesuit priests continued to practise the old rites in secret; they hid in the houses of sympathizers and in specially built priests' holes in some country houses. In churches, familiar ritual involving incense, burning candles and monastic chant gave way to plainsong and long, tedious sermons. This was not to everyone's liking and congregations began to decline.

QUEEN ELIZABETH I

'The Lady Elizabeth shines like a star.'

Foreign ambassador
visiting Elizabeth I's Court

A ROYAL PRESENT

While in her teens, Elizabeth commissioned this portrait of herself as a present for her father King Henry, ensuring that it portrayed her as a serious and scholarly young princess.

ELIZABETH'S CHILDHOOD was turbulent. Her birth, on 7 September 1533, was a huge disappointment to her parents, who longed only for a boy. In May 1536, just two days before she was beheaded, Henry had his marriage with Anne dissolved. At the same time Elizabeth was declared a bastard, excluded from the succession and kept at a safe distance from Henry.

In October 1537 her half-brother Edward was born. Both children were given the best tutors and a similar education. By the age of ten the little princess was being coached in Italian, French and Latin. Later she took up Greek as well. This early training was to prove invaluable to Elizabeth since her councillors and her courtiers could not but respect the opinions of a queen who was able, on the spur of the moment, to berate the Polish ambassador in fluent and faultless Latin!

When Henry died in January 1547 Elizabeth was 13 years old and her brother only nine. Edward's mentors were wholeheartedly committed to furthering the Protestant cause. Elizabeth accepted the government's lead, but her half-sister Mary did not. And so Mary became the hope of the conservatives and Catholics, while the Protestants began to look to Elizabeth should Edward die before becoming a man, which seemed ever more likely. As Mary's policies unfolded, Elizabeth became the repository of the hopes of all the discontented, who began to take comfort from the knowledge that Mary was childless and that Elizabeth would, in time, succeed. Some, however, such as Thomas Wyatt were not content to wait for her succession. In January 1554 Wyatt rose in rebellion against Mary's proposed marriage with Philip. Letters from Wyatt to Elizabeth were discovered and the princess was sent to the Tower under grave suspicion of treason. If Elizabeth had ever answered Wyatt it must have been by word of mouth, because no proof of criminal complicity was to be found. Elizabeth escaped, but learned the value of discretion. Elizabeth's accession in 1558 was greeted with joyous acclaim by Court and commoner alike.

Elizabeth quickly perceived the immensity of the task ahead of her. Under Mary, England had joined Spain in war against France, and the nation's finances were in dire straits: the currency was debased, inflation was rampant and living standards were falling. It is to Elizabeth's credit that she never evaded the issues. The lessons of her upbringing – caution, discretion, avoiding extravagance or high-risk strategies – were to stand her in good stead. She avoided confrontation with her Council and Parliament, listened to advice, was influenced by popular opinion and was acutely conscious of how she was perceived both at home and abroad.

ANOINTING SPOON
This spoon was used to anoint Elizabeth during her coronation on 15 January, a date chosen by John Dee, later appointed as her official Court Astrologer.

'GOD HATH RAISED ME HIGH'
So said Elizabeth, bedecked in coronation robes, at the ceremony at Westminster Abbey in the early spring of 1559, crowning her Queen of all England.

CORONATION SERVICE BOOK
This richly illustrated service book was used at Elizabeth I's coronation, a joyous occasion heralding the beginning of a successful 45-year reign.

CRUCIAL TO THE SMOOTH running of Elizabeth's kingdom were the members of her Privy Council, and she consistently chose wisely. They, in turn, served her admirably and faithfully, often for many years. The three key appointments were Secretary of State, Lord Chancellor and Lord Treasurer. Between them, the holders of these posts guided home and foreign policy, legal matters and the financial affairs of the kingdom.

William Cecil, later Lord Burghley, remained a member of her Council for 40 years, firstly as Secretary of State and then as Lord Treasurer. Cecil was astute, hardworking and utterly trustworthy. A university-trained lawyer, he was typical of the new breed, assuming power at a time when the influence of the Church and the aristocracy on government was declining. Only one cleric, Archbishop John Whitgift, served on the Council during Elizabeth's entire reign, and the aristocracy lacked the necessary learning. According to Thomas More, the Duke of Norfolk would have 'snored through the Sermon on the Mount', while the 1st Earl of Pembroke, who served on Elizabeth's initial Council, was illiterate. In contrast, Francis Walsingham, Privy Councillor and later Secretary of State, and Nicholas Bacon, also a prominent Privy Councillor, had

'You will give me that council that you think best.'

Queen Elizabeth to William Cecil, when appointing him her Principal Secretary of State

THE SPYMASTER

Sir Francis Walsingham was firstly a member of the Privy Council and then a Secretary of State. He instigated the nation's secret service, with a network of spies at home and abroad.

QUEEN AND PARLIAMENT

This picture shows Elizabeth at the State Opening of Parliament at Westminster. Parliament was becoming progressively more powerful and the queen was always respectful and courteous when dealing with its members.

studied at university, as had Robert Cecil and Francis Bacon who followed in their fathers' footsteps.

Robert Cecil, who became Secretary of State in 1596, was small and hunchbacked with a brilliant mind, but he was devious, deceitful and unpopular, being particularly disliked by his arch-rival, Robert Devereux, 2nd Earl of Essex. Nevertheless, despite constant individual rivalries, notably between William Cecil and Robert Dudley, Earl of Leicester, the Council served the queen superbly throughout

her reign, not least because it included an admirable balance of hawks and doves: some, like William Cecil, urged caution and others, like Dudley and Walsingham, favoured a more aggressive stance. Elizabeth was quick to take credit for her Council's decisions, except when this might make her unpopular, as with the execution of Mary Queen of Scots. Mary, a Catholic, had become a dangerous focus of insurrection. In 1587, when given Mary's death warrant by her Secretary, Sir William Davison, Elizabeth had signed it. Then, on discovering that the Council had executed Mary, she became hysterical and consigned Davison to the Tower.

CECIL AND SON

'I mean to direct all my actions by good advice and council.' Thus spoke the queen. William and Robert Cecil were Elizabeth's key councillors: William was appointed at the beginning of her reign; his son, Robert, was in office when she died.

ADVISE AND CONSENT

Andre Hurault de Maisse, a perceptive French Ambassador, provides a unique insight into the relationship between Queen Elizabeth and her Council towards the end of her reign. 'Her Government is fairly pleasing to the people who show that they love her,' he records, at the same time commenting, **'she thinks highly of herself and has little regard for the Council, being of the opinion that she is far wiser than they are.'** On the other hand de Maisse discovers, **'When some expense is necessary, her government must deceive her before embarking on it little by little.'** De Maisse conveys an intimate first-hand account of the relationship between an ageing queen and the progressively more confident Privy Council.

AS SOON AS ELIZABETH had ascended the throne, her newly appointed Council urged her to marry, out of a desire to see the queen produce a healthy male heir who would maintain the Tudor dynasty. 'God send our mistress a husband and by time a son so that we may hope our posterity shall have a masculine successor,' prayed William Cecil.

THE DANCING QUEEN
Elizabeth was both an enthusiastic and expert dancer to the end of her life. Here she dances the popular La Volta with her long-time favourite Robert Dudley, later Earl of Leicester.

The queen, however, was reluctant to oblige, although she was certainly not short of suitors. She was young and attractive and the prospect of becoming her consort was dazzling. The cream of

English aristocracy and foreign royalty flocked to Court to vie for her favours. Their attentions were greatly enjoyed by the queen, who adored flattery, particularly when it was bestowed by the most powerful men in Europe.

Elizabeth preferred her men to be tall, dark and handsome. Robert Dudley (later Earl of Leicester), Christopher Hatton and Walter Raleigh were all cast in this mould but they wooed her in vain. Unlike her father, Elizabeth never let her heart rule her head, astutely realizing that marrying one of her own countrymen could

severely upset the others. Dudley was without doubt her one great love but he was already married and, when his wife died in suspicious circumstances, Elizabeth was afraid to continue the relationship in case it tarnished her reputation. Hatton never married and, in 1592, Raleigh was sent to the Tower briefly when he fell in love with Bess Throckmorton, one of the queen's maids of honour, whom he later married.

As for suitors from abroad, too many were Catholic and such a marriage would have made Elizabeth as unpopular as her half-sister Mary had been. Archduke Charles of Austria would not renounce his Catholicism and the effeminate Prince Henry of Anjou was 'obstinately papist-ical'. Even the Pope murmured, ''Tis a pity Elizabeth and I cannot marry, our children would have ruled the world.' Elizabeth would have none of them. She had developed a liking for the consummate power of being queen of England and did not want to share this privilege with anyone else – particularly a husband.

The only man who came near to marrying the queen was Hercules-François, Duke of Alençon and younger brother of Henry of Anjou. Despite his shortcomings, she was entranced, calling him 'my little frog' and praising his charm, wit and political astuteness. Marriage negotiations were conducted at Warwick Castle – but to no avail.

Robert Devereux, 2nd Earl of Essex, and stepson of Robert Dudley, was the last in a long line of handsome young men who became Elizabeth's favourites. Impossibly arrogant and over-ambitious, Essex attracted the animosity of Robert Cecil and of Raleigh. He was accused of treason after leading an ill-conceived rebellion against the queen and was executed at the Tower of London in February 1601.

HOME OF THE EARL OF LEICESTER
Elizabeth gave Kenilworth Castle to Robert Dudley who entertained the queen here on numerous occasions. Now a magnificent ruin, it is in the care of English Heritage.

THE 'LITTLE FROG'
The Duke of Alençon, the Frenchman that Elizabeth was tempted to marry.

ELIZABETHAN SEA CAPTAINS AND ADVENTURERS

ALTHOUGH HENRY VIII HAD built up a fine navy, England had seemed for a time to be less eager than the Spanish and Portuguese to discover new horizons. In Elizabethan England, however, brave sea captains set sail to explore uncharted seas and new lands, or to seize rich pickings on the Spanish Main.

Between 1576 and 1578 Martin Frobisher made three attempts to discover a route to China via the North-West Passage. Humphrey Gilbert claimed Newfoundland for the queen in 1583 but perished on the voyage home when his small ship *Squirrel* disappeared beneath the storm-tossed Atlantic. In 1585 Raleigh established the first English settlement in the Americas, named Virginia in honour of the Virgin Queen. A series of voyages by John Hawkins and Francis Drake to the Caribbean, undertaken between 1562 and 1584, effectively challenged the long-standing Spanish monopoly of the New World by continually attacking their ships and settlements.

It was not all plain sailing. Life aboard ship for ordinary seamen was harsh and highly dangerous. They slept on deck, ate rotting meat and biscuits full of weevils. When supplies ran low they could be put ashore or cast adrift. Discipline was ruthless – Drake once punished the ship's chaplain because he did not like the sermon. Scurvy and typhus posed a constant threat. Drake took five ships on

AN ELIZABETHAN HERO

Martin Frobisher made several heroic yet fruitless voyages, trying to discover a north-west passage to the Orient. He was later knighted at sea for his services against the Armada.

THE SHIPBUILDERS

Elizabethan shipwrights at work in the Royal Dockyard. John Hawkins oversaw a massive overhaul of the Queen's Fleet, which was completed in time for the Armada in 1588.

'To seek new worlds, for gold, for praise, for glory.'
                                    Sir Walter Raleigh

DRAKE'S SHIP
A contemporary drawing by Hulsius shows the Golden Hind *in the act of capturing a Spanish treasure galleon off the coast of South America.*

THE MONARCH'S MINDER
Sir Walter Raleigh, resplendent in Greenwich armour, as Captain of the Guard. Appointed in 1587, he was responsible for the queen's personal safety.

his epic voyage 'around the whole Globe' in 1577. Three years later, only the *Golden Hind* returned to Plymouth Sound with just half of its original crew still surviving.

There were few charts and navigation was primitive. Life could end slowly in a Spanish dungeon, or swiftly when struck by an iceberg, poisoned arrow or musket ball. Most sea captains died with their sea-boots on and were buried at sea. Richard Grenville met an heroic death when hopelessly outnumbered by a Spanish fleet off the Azores in 1591 and Frobisher was mortally wounded fighting against the Spaniards off the French coast in 1594. Both Drake and Hawkins died of dysentery in 1596 while on yet another expedition to the Caribbean; Drake's body lies in a lead coffin in the warm waters off Panama: 'The trumpets sound in doleful manner echoing out their lamentation for so great a loss and all the cannon in the fleet discharged.'

SEA MONSTER

'The same day, at a south-west sunne, **there was a monstrous Whale aboard of us, so neare to our side that we might have thrust a sworde or any other weapon in him,** which we durst not doe for feare hee should have overthrown our shippe: and then I called my company together, and all of us shouted, and with the crie we made he departed from us.'
                                    Principal Navigations, Richard Hakluyt

DRAKE AND THE ARMADA

RELATIONS BETWEEN ENGLAND and Spain progressively worsened under Elizabeth. Provocative acts such as Drake's plundering in the New World and his strike on Spanish shipping at Cadiz in 1587, the famous 'singeing of the king's beard', made the Spanish king determined to exact retribution. Driven by his desire to restore England to the 'true faith', Europe's most powerful Catholic monarch launched the Armada, then the mightiest fleet ever to threaten English shores: 'the ocean groaning under the weight of them,' wrote historian William Camden.

Elizabeth had shrewdly appointed Lord Howard of Effingham as her Lord High Admiral, Drake as Vice Admiral and Hawkins as Rear Admiral. Howard was widely respected and proved capable of controlling the swashbuckling buccaneers who were his captains. Conversely Philip II of Spain's choice of the Duke of Medina Sidona as 'Captain General of the Ocean Seas' was a serious error. The Duke possessed no maritime experience or leadership qualities and, moreover, suffered from acute seasickness.

Hawkins, as Navy Treasurer, had modernized the English ships so that they were quicker and manoeuvred better than the huge, lumbering Spanish galleons, which were ideal for long voyages but hopelessly unsuited to the

A CRUCIAL BATTLE

The mighty Spanish Armada, under attack from the English fleet and shallow-draught Dutch cromships during the summer of 1588.

A TIMELY WARNING

As soon as the Spanish Armada was first seen off The Lizard in Cornwall, a chain of beacons was lit all along the shore to warn of its approach.

confined waters of the English Channel. Furthermore, the traditional Spanish tactics of going alongside their adversaries and boarding them with heavily armed soldiers were frustrated by the nimbler English ships steering clear and bombarding the enemy with cannon fire. Most importantly the English were in home waters and, unlike the Spanish, had an intimate knowledge of the complex tides, currents and winds.

When the Spanish Armada arrived off the Cornish coast, Howard's fleet was at Plymouth, trapped by unfavourable wind and tide while revictualling after a foray into the Western Approaches. Thus there was a marvellous opportunity for Medina to avenge Spain's humiliation at Cadiz the previous year, but instead the ultra cautious and inexperienced Medina spurned a unique chance to destroy the English fleet at anchor.

The English were able to creep out at nightfall on the ebb tide, get windward of the Armada and engage the Spanish ships the following day. There was no single decisive battle. Instead there was a series of inconclusive running skirmishes as the Armada wafted majestically up the Channel to rendezvous with the Duke of Parma's army at Calais. Here Medina committed another mistake by anchoring, so enabling Drake to send in fireships. The confused Spaniards fled home via Scotland and Ireland, suffering terrible losses from the savage storms and treacherous coastlines. The English did not lose a single ship.

GLORIANA

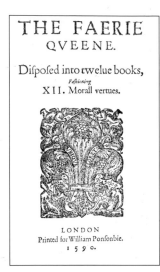

THE FAERIE
QVEENE.

Difpofed into twelue books,
Fashioning
XII. Morall vertues.

LONDON
Printed for William Ponfonbie.
1590.

SONG OF PRAISE

The Faerie Queene was written by Edmund Spenser as a tribute to Elizabeth. 'Her angel face, as the great eye of heaven shines bright, and made a sunshine in the shady place.'

THE RESOUNDING DEFEAT of the Spanish Armada in 1588 made England a front-rank power and elevated Elizabeth to universal acclaim as the 'Sun Queen'. Two years later, the first three volumes of Edmund Spenser's *The Faerie Queene* were published, in which Elizabeth was portrayed as Gloriana. Admirers flocked to praise the queen and the nation basked in a new sense of pride and purpose, a feeling of greatness and glory, as England became a land of achievement and opportunity in the rapidly expanding world of the 16th century.

George Gower's striking 'Armada' portrait sums up Elizabeth's achievements. This iconographic neo-medieval portrait depicts the queen magnificently dressed in a heavily embroidered velvet and satin gown, with huge puffed sleeves, lace ruff and cascades of pearls. Her hand rests imperiously on the globe, immaculately manicured fingernails pointing symbolically at Virginia, while behind her the Spanish fleet is depicted sailing towards its doom. Thus is captured the euphoria of the queen and her kingdom after the resounding defeat of a powerful enemy.

Although the war with Spain continued, the sense of peril had abated. The victory over the Spanish Armada had been their finest hour. The queen was to live a further 15 years but it was the Armada defeat that established her reputation as one of Europe's greatest monarchs. Elizabeth's public image

remained untarnished, and this was the great secret of her success. She was expert at presenting herself to her people in the best light. She made repeated public progresses through her kingdom and displayed a genuine interest in the welfare of even the meanest of her subjects as she passed. Impromptu speeches to the thronging spectators, the good-humoured receiving of even the coarsest but well-intentioned gesture of goodwill, the spectacle of majesty riding in state in a litter borne by noblemen contributed to the legend of this great English queen.

Elizabeth could rightly be proud of her achievements during a reign that had spanned almost half a century. Queen in a man's world, Elizabeth's skilful handling of strong men and slender resources slowly but surely fashioned England into a great nation. She had firmly established Protestantism as the national church, thereby avoiding the sectarian wars that bedevilled France and other European countries, and had led England to a great victory against Spain, the mightiest power in Europe, in a manner which gained for both herself and the kingdom the admiration of the rest of the civilized world.

A VICTORY MEDAL

The Armada Jewel features a miniature portrait of Queen Elizabeth and commemorates the defeat of the Spanish Armada. It is now in the Victoria and Albert Museum, London.

'Did never mortal eye behold such heavenly grace.' The Faerie Queene, *Edmund Spenser*

THE 'ARMADA' PORTRAIT

George Gower's portrait of Queen Elizabeth. This painting hangs in the Long Gallery at Woburn Abbey, the home of the Duke of Bedford. Ironically it sits alongside her long-time adversary, Philip, King of Spain.

The Succession

THE QUEEN IS DEAD

Elizabeth's funeral took place on 28 April 1603. The service was conducted by the Archbishop of Canterbury, John Whitgift, who the queen had called her 'little black husband'.

IN THE EARLY SPRING of 1603, when the queen was in her 70th year, she caught a chill. As her condition worsened, Elizabeth stubbornly refused to retire to her bed. Instead she sat in silence on a pile of cushions in front of the fire, staring into the flames. 'Your Majesty, to content the people you must go to bed,' advised her Secretary of State, Robert Cecil. 'Little man, is "must" a word to be addressed to princes?' was Elizabeth's tart rejoinder.

The wily Sir Robert Cecil had for some time been anticipating Elizabeth's death and, mindful of his own political future, had been secretly negotiating for James VI

'Here I sit and govern with my pen that with which others only attempted with the sword.' King James I

'IN MY END IS MY BEGINNING'

Accused of plotting to seize the English throne, Mary Queen of Scots was brought down to the Great Hall of Fotheringay Castle in Lincolnshire early in the morning of the 8 February 1587. Attired in sober black satin, she ascended the scaffold in complete silence, watched by a gawping crowd of country gentry who had gathered to witness the execution. Mary then disrobed for the execution, revealing a scarlet bodice and petticoat. Silhouetted blood red – the Catholic colour of martyrdom – against the black cloth-covered scaffold, she knelt to await the axe. After two swift blows her wig fell off and the executioner held up the head of an ageing woman. A small, whimpering dog crawled out from beneath the bloodstained corpse.

of Scotland to become James I of England and Scotland. James was Elizabeth's cousin and there was no real alternative, particularly if the nation was to remain firmly Protestant – Lord Burghley had even contemplated England becoming a republic if all else failed. The queen died at Richmond in the early hours of 24 March 1603, after indicating that she wished her cousin, James VI of Scotland, the son of Mary Queen of Scots, to be her successor.

So in the spring of 1603 the unthinkable occurred – a Scotsman ascended the English throne, not by force of arms but by invitation. Edward I, 'the Hammer of the Scots', would be turning in his grave, Robert the Bruce greatly amused, and Mary Queen of Scots, who had been executed for plotting to seize the English throne, would surely have smirked. For his part, James accepted the English Crown with alacrity and was soon on the long journey south to claim his new kingdom and be welcomed with open arms. 'By nyne of the clocke James the Kinge of Scotlande was pclaimed in London to be oure Kinge ... at which tyme here was greate trivmphe with Bondfiers, gunnes and ringinge of bells with other kinds of musicke.'

MOTHER AND SON

James was destined to follow his mother onto the Scottish throne as King James VI, and later to succeed Elizabeth as James I of England. Although this portrait shows James with Mary, Mary never saw her son after he was taken from her when he was ten months old.

THE TUDOR ERA DEVELOPED into an age of opulence, exuberance and extravagance, fully reflected in the architecture and the social activity of the time. Out of the stately but sober reign of Henry VII came a desire to dazzle and impress. Tudor monarchs wanted to upstage their Continental rivals and excite influential foreign visitors. Henry VIII, in particular, was greatly envious of the fabulous chateaux of his arch-rival, French king François I, who employed Leonardo da Vinci as his architect. Henry was determined to build something even more imposing in England.

Rich Tudor courtiers, many of them self-made men, also wished to flaunt their new-found wealth by building houses which were enormous compared with those of the Middle Ages. Elizabeth's most ambitious courtiers sought the ultimate accolade of entertaining the queen in their own home, although this could prove to be a costly enterprise.

The main function of the Tudor royal palace was to accommodate the monarch's household in suitably grandiose surroundings and provide the stage for the Royal Court to perform. The Court was the centre of power but it was also a place of dreams, romance, intrigue, naked ambition, treachery, success and abject failure. Here fortunes could be won, a place in the sun secured.

The Court was, however, a rollercoaster: those riding high in royal esteem could suddenly be plunged to their doom. At the Royal Court success was priceless but failure could be fatal, as More, Cromwell, Anne Boleyn, Catherine Howard and Essex all learned to their cost.

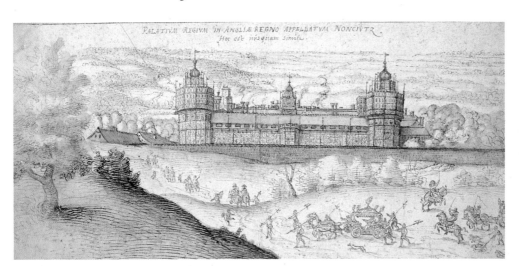

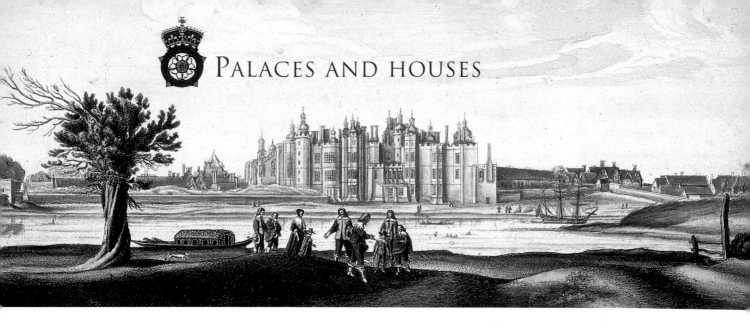

PALACES AND HOUSES

THE FIRST TUDOR PALACE
Built by Henry VII, shortly after he acquired the throne, Richmond Palace remained a royal favourite throughout the Tudor age until Elizabeth died there in 1603.

GARDEN TAPESTRY
One of the Stoke Edith needlework hangings at Montacute in Somerset, a Tudor house now owned by The National Trust. It depicts a typical Elizabethan garden.

AFTER THE WARS OF THE ROSES there was little need for monarchs to live in a castle. In pursuit of greater comfort and to accommodate their huge army of retainers, the Tudor monarchs built impressive palaces that projected the power and prestige of the monarchy. Henry VII built Richmond Palace, named after his earldom, and it became a popular royal residence throughout the Tudor era: his granddaughter Elizabeth called it her 'warm little box'. Today all that is left is the old palace gatehouse bearing Henry's coat of arms.

Another favourite palace of Henry VII's was Greenwich, which he refaced with red brick; both Henry VIII and Elizabeth were born there. Henry VII also completed St George's Chapel at Windsor Castle,

which like the Tower of London had been a royal residence for many centuries. Further away, near Oxford, lay the Manor of Woodstock and a house, later the site of Blenheim Palace.

Henry VIII possessed more than 50 palaces and lavished vast sums of money on them – £2.5 million at Whitehall, acquired from Cardinal Wolsey and covering 26 acres beside the River Thames, £18.5 million at Hampton Court and £7.5 million at Nonsuch in Surrey. Only two of Henry VIII's palaces – St James's in London and Hampton Court – have substantially survived.

The new breed of successful self-made men in Elizabethan England, wishing to display the wealth that they had acquired, created houses that were confident, assertive and stylish. Such residences belatedly introduced the Renaissance into England and established the home as a status symbol par excellence. Burghley House, in East Anglia, took William Cecil more than 30 years to construct and was later described by Daniel Defoe as 'more like a town than a house'. Longleat, near Bath, was begun by John Thynne, a former

clerk in Edward VI's royal kitchen. It was completed during Elizabeth's reign and the queen was lavishly entertained there in 1574. Today Longleat is widely considered to be an outstanding example of English Renaissance architecture.

The dissolution of the monasteries had provided substantial amounts of money, land and building materials to be put to new use. This led to some interesting property conversions whereby the former abbeys at Buckland in Devon, Anglesey near Cambridge, Woburn in Bedfordshire and Wilton in Wiltshire were all transformed into residences for illustrious Elizabethans. Sudeley Castle in the Cotswolds, the last home of Catherine Parr, where Elizabeth lived for a brief time, was greatly enlarged using building material taken from nearby Winchcombe Abbey. Elizabeth's other childhood home, Hatfield Palace, where she held her first Privy Council, was later opulently rebuilt by one of her most successful ministers, Robert Cecil.

A TUDOR MASTERPIECE
The Green Bedchamber at Hardwick Hall in Derbyshire, built by Bess of Hardwick, the richest woman in England after Queen Elizabeth.

'The cloud capped towers, the gorgeous palaces.'

A foreign visitor to England after seeing several of the royal palaces

TUDOR RENAISSANCE MANSION
Longleat in Wiltshire was built by John Thynne, who was knighted by Henry VIII and entertained Queen Elizabeth.

HENRY VIII's COURT

> ## 'This magnificent, excellent and triumphant Court.'
>
> *A foreign ambassador, on visiting Henry VIII's Court*

HENRY'S COURT WAS JUST like the king – impressive, extravagant and larger than life. Henry believed that his Royal Court should symbolize the strength, status and wealth of his kingdom; it was to be majestic, awe-inspiring, even intimidating, to foreign visitors. To this end no expense was spared.

Henry possessed prodigious energy, rising at dawn, hunting all day and partying well into the night, with feasting, dancing and all manner of entertainment – the king was an accomplished musician and a graceful dancer. Being a member of the Court could be both exhausting and expensive: a courtier had to look the part which meant having fine clothes and a well-filled purse. The king was a compulsive gambler and courtiers had to be prepared to be high rollers; many were severely in debt when they died, as indeed was the king.

Henry's Court was predominantly male. Out of an average complement of well over 1,000, less than 100 were women – even the less attractive ones could be sure

of plenty of attention! Not surprisingly, a considerable change in this male-dominated scenario would take place after Henry died and his daughters succeeded to the throne. The king had 18 gentlemen of the Privy Chamber and six grooms. These were later replaced by eight gentlewomen of the Privy Chamber together with ladies-in-waiting and an assortment of maids of honour, who had come to Court to acquire a wealthy, well-known husband. Both Anne Boleyn and Jane Seymour had been maids of honour when they attracted Henry's notoriously roving eye, as had Bessie Blount, the mistress who bore the king an illegitimate son, later created the Duke of Richmond.

Courtiers could expect to have their lodgings provided together with food and drink according to their station, along with other essentials such as candles and firewood. A member of the Court might have an impressive title, Master of the King's Revels, Master of the King's Horse, Gentleman Pensioner, Esquire of the Body Extraordinary or Groom of the Stool. The last named was closest to the king,

performing the most intimate of duties for the monarch. Henry Norris was the king's Groom of the Stool for a time, but Henry suspected him of intimacy with Anne Boleyn and had him executed. The Court, under the overall control of the Lord Chamberlain, was divided into the King's Side and the Queen's Side, each with its own extensive household. The king's inner sanctum was the Privy Chamber, its more prominent members locked in a continual power struggle, with fortunes fluctuating according to the relative strengths of the rival factions. Thus Henry's Court was a powerful magnet to ambitious men seeking patronage and an opportunity for personal advancement. The stakes were high, the competition intense, the chances of success completely unpredictable.

HAMPTON COURT AND THE THAMES

'Why come ye not to Court?
To which court?
To the king's court or Hampton Court?
Nay, to the king's court
The king's court should have excellence
but Hampton Court hath the pre-eminence.'

*A skit by the poet John Skelton, at a time when Hampton Court
was owned by Cardinal Wolsey*

THOMAS WOLSEY GAVE King Henry Hampton Court Palace in 1528, in an attempt to appease Henry's growing displeasure with him. It was already a palace of great splendour: Wolsey's success and power had brought him immense wealth and at Hampton Court he built a palace that would reflect his own glory and power. As soon as Henry acquired Hampton Court, however, he began to rebuild and enlarge it to make it possibly the most opulent of all his palaces.

HAMPTON COURT KITCHENS
This kitchen at Hampton Court Palace has been recreated as it was in Tudor times. Henry VIII's larger kitchens consisted of more than 50 rooms.

HAMPTON COURT GATEWAY
Henry VIII's coat of arms are carved into a panel above the central gateway into Hampton Court Palace, a showpiece of opulence and pleasure.

REAL TENNIS

Real (or royal) tennis, newly taken up by the aristocracy, was regularly played at Hampton Court, particularly by Henry VIII. **'He is extremely fond of tennis, at which game it is the prettiest thing in the world to see him play, his fair skin glowing through a shirt of the finest texture,'** enthused an excited spectator as the king bounded gracefully around the court, striking the ball with power and precision. Spectators bet heavily on the outcome of matches; Anne Boleyn was watching a game when guards hustled her away to imprisonment in the Tower, with Anne complaining loudly that she had not yet had time to collect her winnings.

THE HAUNTED GALLERY

It is said that the ghost of the doomed Catherine Howard, Henry VIII's fifth wife, appears on occasions shrieking hysterically in this gallery.

Henry built a new Great Hall, remodelled the Chapel Royal and greatly enlarged the kitchens in order to feed the thousand and more members of the Court that accompanied him when he was in residence. All of these rooms still exist today and the Great Hall, with its soaring hammer-beam roof, contains a superb painting of the Field of Cloth of Gold (shown on page 14), one of the most important Tudor works of art remaining in the Royal Collection.

Elizabeth used Hampton Court infrequently as it had unhappy memories – her half-sister Mary once held her prisoner in the Water Gallery and, in the autumn of 1562, Elizabeth nearly died of smallpox here. Hampton Court continues to be most closely associated with Henry VIII.

The palace lies on the banks of the River Thames which in the 16th century provided the main transport link with other royal palaces downstream such as Richmond, St James's, Whitehall and Greenwich. The magnificent astronomical clock above the gateway to Clock Court shows the time of high water at London Bridge, vital information when wafting down the river on the royal barge.

TALL CHIMNEYS

The tall, elaborately worked brick chimneys at Hampton Court Palace are typical of those on large buildings built during the Tudor period, combining both an imposing appearance and practicality.

ELIZABETH'S COURT

IN ELIZABETHAN ENGLAND the Royal Court was the centre of power and influence in the kingdom. Men of ambition were attracted to it by the possibility of fame and fortune, and the chance of catching the queen's attention. Colourful courtiers, from privy councillors, peers of the realm and senior Court officials to young opportunists, revolved around the monarch like so many planets orbiting the sun.

Like Henry, Elizabeth loved hunting and all manner of entertainment. 'She took the crossbow and killed six does and she did me the honour to give me a share of them,' marvelled the French ambassador at Woodstock Palace when the queen was well into middle age. She had also inherited Henry VIII's red hair, fiery temper and restless energy: the Court, like a huge travelling circus, scurried endlessly

ROYAL COMMAND PERFORMANCE

Elizabeth was an avid supporter of the theatre and of William Shakespeare in particular, who put on many private productions for the queen – her favourite play was supposedly The Merry Wives of Windsor.

'IF MUSIC BE THE FOOD OF LOVE ...'

Elizabeth's virginals; small harpsichords like the one shown here were very popular in the 16th and 17th centuries and the queen was a proficient player.

COURT RIVALRIES

Friction could easily develop in the hothouse atmosphere of the Tudor Royal Court, particularly between ambitious newcomers and the old aristocracy, anxious to protect its power base from unwelcome intrusion. Thus the Duke of Norfolk contemptuously condemned Thomas Cromwell as **'unfit to meddle with the affairs of kings'**, whilst the lofty Earl of Essex looked down on the diminutive Robert Cecil as an upstart. The unrepentant Cecil riposted by adopting the motto for his coat of arms, *Sero sed serio* ('Late but in earnest'). Essex was beheaded; Cecil was created the 1st Earl of Salisbury.

> *'When she smiled it was pure sunshine that everyone did choose to bask in if they could, but anon came a storm and thunder fell in wondrous manner on all alike.'*
>
> Sir John Harington, a prominent courtier and Elizabeth's godson

between Hampton Court, Whitehall, Richmond, Nonsuch, Windsor, Hatfield and other royal palaces.

In summer Elizabeth conducted royal progresses around the kingdom during which she and her entourage would be entertained at colossal expense in the palatial homes of her wealthier courtiers. These progresses, like those of earlier monarchs, demonstrated the grandeur of the sovereign and impressed her subjects. Similarly, annual ceremonies such as the Order of the Knight of the Garter processions at Windsor and the Accession Day tournaments were occasions of great royal splendour: the queen surrounded by devoted knights competing for favours.

Elizabeth was an accomplished musician on a variety of instruments. She could also sing well and greatly enjoyed dancing, especially the gaillard, a quick, lively dance, featuring a spectacular leap in the air 'after the Florentine style'.

While the Court was entertained by masques, banquets, theatrical performances and musical extravaganzas, Elizabeth would invariably retire to study state papers. Messengers could arrive at all hours and the Privy Council was constantly on call for late-night consultations with the queen. The Royal Court had the appearance of a living theatre with Elizabeth always centre stage.

WHEN KNIGHTS WERE BOLD

A Tudor tiltyard for jousting tournaments, complete with elaborate judge's box. This was an ideal occasion for courtiers to display their courage and prowess, thereby catching the royal eye.

INTRODUCING THE JOUST

By Elizabeth's reign, tournaments began with much colourful ceremony and stirring speeches, some written by professional speech writers like Francis Bacon who wrote for the Earl of Essex.

ROYAL PROCESSIONS

PROCESSION TO BLACKFRIARS

This colourful painting by Robert Peake, c.1600, vividly portrays the elaborate processions of Elizabeth's reign, the queen being carried by her Knights of the Garter.

'WHEN THE QUEEN GOES abroad in public the Lord Chamberlain walks first, being followed by all the nobility who are in Court, and the Knights of the Order that are present walk after, near the Queen's person, such as the Earl of Essex, the Admiral and others. After come the six heralds who bear maces before the Queen. After her march the fifty Gentlemen of the Guard, each carrying a halbard, and

sumptuously attired, and after that the Maids and Ladies who accompanied them very well attired.' So wrote Andre Hurault de Maisse, the young and impressionable envoy of the French king to the Court of Queen Elizabeth I, towards the end of the 16th century. His diaries provide a vivid insight into the glamorous world of the Court, a world full of light, colour and spectacle. The Elizabethans loved dressing up in gorgeous costumes and parading in all their finery: they adored pageantry and spectacular entertainment. Courtiers such as Drake, Raleigh and the Earl of Essex were the celebrities of the day, recognized and fêted wherever they went.

Elizabeth's famous summertime royal progresses were really a shrewd public relations exercise to let her be seen amongst her people in favourable circumstances, to meet and greet in the manner of modern-day celebrity walkabouts. Unlike her sister Mary, Elizabeth possessed the common touch and thrived on being the centre of attention. The Spanish Ambassador's account of a royal progress in 1668 neatly encapsulates the moment: 'She was received everywhere with great acclamations and signs of joy, as is customary in this country; whereat she was extremely pleased and told me so, giving me to understand how beloved she was by her subjects and how highly she esteemed this, together with the fact that they were peaceful and contented, whilst

her neighbours on all sides are in such trouble. She attributed it all to God's miraculous goodness. She ordered her carriage sometimes to be taken where the crowd seemed thickest, and stood up and thanked the people.'

The queen and her perceptive Privy Council shrewdly realized the value of such events to demonstrate royal power and favourably influence public opinion. Thus everyday activities such as the monarch going to church were transformed into spectacular productions to dazzle and delight all who observed them, bringing colour into the lives of ordinary people and making them feel part of something special, extras in the glittering world of Gloriana.

A ROYAL HUNT

Elizabeth was passionate about hunting and hawking in which she participated enthusiastically until late in her life. The grounds of the palace at Nonsuch were a particularly favourite venue.

FIT FOR A QUEEN

One of a set of tapestries commissioned by the Earl of Leicester for the queen's apartment at Kenilworth, which she frequently visited.

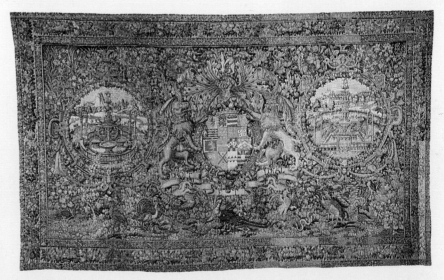

63

Little Moreton Hall near Congleton in Cheshire epitomizes an affluent Tudor dwelling. Once the property of the Moretons, 16th-century wealthy landowners, it is now owned by The National Trust.

A TUDOR TOWN

A picture in the British Library shows the town of Great Yarmouth in Norfolk during the 16th century.

TUDOR TREES

Illustrations of trees taken from a Tudor pattern book in the Bodleian Library, part of Oxford University. This library is named after Sir Thomas Bodley, a wealthy Elizabethan diplomat and scholar.

THE FUNDAMENTAL CHANGES that swept across the Tudor kingdom affected the lives of all its inhabitants from the highest to the most humble of its citizens. The nation's religious allegiance was changed from traditional Roman Catholicism to the new Protestant faith and for the first time the Bible could be read in English. The population expanded greatly during the Tudor era and it became progressively more urbanized. Inflation was the bane of Tudor England: prices doubled between 1540 and 1548, continuing to rise steeply during Elizabeth's reign. The rich grew richer, the new middle class tasted affluence, yet more than half of the population remained in poverty.

Society became more sophisticated in terms of houses, food, clothes and leisure activities, yet hygiene and medicine remained medieval, deadly diseases such as bubonic plague periodically decimating the population. Communications, too, had improved little since the Middle Ages. The roads outside the towns were little more than dust tracks in summer, while in winter they became virtually impassable. The only means of transport was on horseback or by boat along the river. Outside London it took days to travel any distance and the queen never went further north than Stafford or west of Bristol.

Above all, in sharp contrast to the days of the Wars of the Roses, England remained largely peaceful. Apart from sporadic skirmishes on the Scottish border and minor rebellions, no significant fighting took place within the kingdom during the whole of the 16th century.

TUDOR PLAYTIME

This stylish Elizabethan pavilion at Montacute House in Somerset was originally used for dining, drinking, gambling and other pleasurable pursuits. Montacute House is now owned by The National Trust.

A FEATURE OF THE TUDOR era was a rapidly expanding and increasingly more affluent middle class, which now included numerous merchants and traders, men such as the successful glover, John Shakespeare, who became an alderman in Stratford-upon-Avon, and his third son, William, the world's greatest dramatist.

Many benefited from the vast amount of land that became widely available after the dissolution of the monasteries: the country gentry prospered mightily, as did the farmers. Trerice, an exquisite manor house in deepest Cornwall, was built in 1573 by rich gentleman farmer Sir John Arundell. Kelmscott Manor in Oxfordshire, later the country home of William Morris, was also originally constructed by a wealthy Elizabethan farmer.

In these favourable circumstances, men such as Thomas Wolsey and Francis Drake rose from obscurity to become eminently successful. William Shakespeare, and theatre owners and impresarios such as James Burbage and Philip Henslowe, thrived as the demand for theatre and entertainment burgeoned during Queen Elizabeth's reign. The Tudors were extremely litigious, so lawyers prospered accordingly. Sir Edward Phelips, Master of the Rolls in the late 16th century, created the beautiful honey-coloured stone house in Somerset known as Montacute. Other properties, such as Athelhampton in Dorset, built right at the beginning of the Tudor period, were also owned by thrusting Tudor entrepreneurs who had thrived in this era of energy and enterprise.

ACES HIGH

Wealthy Tudor gamblers are depicted here playing a card game called primero. Judging by their serious expressions and large piles of coins, they must be playing for high stakes!

But not everybody prospered. The gap between rich and poor widened markedly. The cost of food and other essential goods required by the average artisan family increased fivefold during the 16th century, and the failure of wages to keep pace with the inflationary spiral contributed to widespread poverty.

Numerous vagrants roamed the country. In 1570 there were 2,000 beggars in Norwich alone, 10 per cent of that city's population. The Elizabethan Poor Laws, by which parishes became responsible for providing basic food and shelter for their own poor, proved unpopular and repressive. The conditions in parish poorhouses were such that only the most needy would enter them. Many better-off Elizabethans, however, gave generously to the poor.

DRIVEN TO BEGGING

Many lowly paid people constantly ran the risk of falling into financial difficulty. Here a Tudor textile worker comments on the effects of a sudden slump in trade:

'Infinite numbers of spinners, carders and pickers of wool are turned to begging, with no small store of poor children, who driven with necessity both come idly about to beg, to the oppression of the poor husbandmen, and rob their hedges of linen, steal pig, goose and capon, steal fruit and corn in the harvest time and rob barns in the winter.'

'Poverty is the father of innumerable infirmities.'

Robert Greene, Elizabethan playwright and one of the 'university wits'

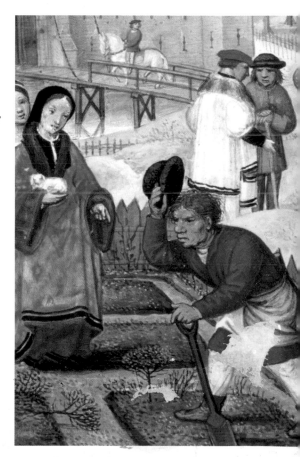

AN ELIZABETHAN FARMHOUSE

Although Kelmscott in the Cotswolds is an Elizabethan manor, much work by William Morris and his Pre-Raphaelite friends can be seen in this house, which is now owned by the Society of Antiquaries.

MORNING MA'AM!

An illustration from The Book of Hours *clearly demonstrates that class differences were respected in Tudor times with due deference.*

Northern Tudor style

Stanley Place in Chester is one of a significant number of distinctive black and white timber-framed buildings that remain from Tudor times.

England's population doubled in the 16th century, while improvements in agriculture allied to a switch from arable to sheep farming which required less labour, began an exodus from the country to the towns. By the end of the century, one fifth of the people lived in towns. London's population had grown to over 300,000, other major towns being Norwich, the main venue of the booming textile trade, Bristol, the second largest port, and York, capital of the north. Elsewhere, Maidstone was twice the size of Manchester, and, whilst Stratford-upon-Avon was a thriving market town, nearby Birmingham was merely a village. Portsmouth and Plymouth were key naval ports and Francis Drake and John Hawkins both had homes there. In northern England, Newcastle was expanding as a commercial port from where coal was shipped south. Elsewhere, this region remained sparsely populated, although Berwick-upon-Tweed was a key garrison frontier town.

This population explosion prompted a massive building programme. The attractive half-timbered buildings in places such as Lavenham, Shrewsbury, Stratford-upon-Avon and Ludlow date back to Tudor times. However, the outwardly attractive appearance of the

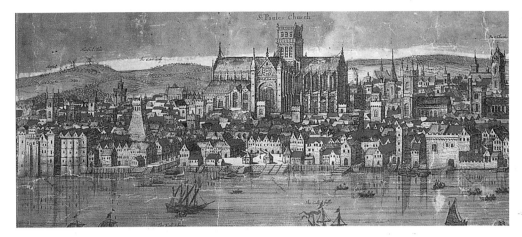

average Tudor dwelling concealed a dark, dingy interior, lit by candles or rush torches. There was no running water or proper drainage and many poorer people lived and cooked in a single, squalid room, while the entire family slept in a room above. 'The floors are commonly of clay strewn with rushes under which lie an ancient collection of beer, grease, fragments of bone, spittle, excrement of dogs and cats and everything that is nasty,' complained Erasmus in 1530. The learned Flemish humanist was the archetypal complainer, moaning about Cambridge's cold, damp climate and the 'raw, small and windy college ale'.

Such cramped and unhygienic living conditions provided a fertile breeding ground for disease, with bubonic plague being a major threat. In 1561 this pestilence raged uncontrollably throughout southern England, killing more than 17,000 people in London alone. Smallpox was equally dreaded and Elizabeth herself nearly died of the disease in 1562. Lady Mary Sidney, who nursed the queen, caught the disease and was so badly pockmarked that she fled the Court. Tudor buildings were also made of highly flammable materials such as wood and straw, so there was a huge risk of fire which could sweep through the closely packed houses and narrow streets with devastating effect. There were no hoses or organized fire brigades so a small fire could quickly become a raging inferno, one of the reasons why only relatively small areas of the original Tudor towns and cities in England continue to exist in present times.

Tudor London

Elizabethan London

South of the Thames in 1588, when this watercolour was painted, was largely open ground. The arenas for animal fights were shortly to be replaced by the Rose and Globe theatres.

London condemned

'All flesh is grass, and all the glory thereof is as the flower of the field': the Puritans did not approve of London, particularly Southwark, whose lurid activities so offended them.

London Bridge

The bridge as it was when William Shakespeare lived and worked in nearby Southwark. Wealthy merchants' houses straddled the entire length of the city's one and only bridge.

THE CAPITAL OF ENGLAND was a pulsating, vibrant city, the centre of government, culture, and above all, a place to do business. The wealthy merchants of the 12 powerful City Guilds conducted their commercial transactions in the newly created Royal Exchange, and their civic affairs at the Guildhall. Their imported goods were transported up the River Thames to quays which stretched from the great fortress of the Tower of London towards Wapping and Limehouse.

Crowded, noisy, dirty and stinking, the capital was spreading rapidly out from the ancient City of London, still with its medieval walls and gates, its skyline dominated by Old St Paul's, later burned down in the Great Fire and considerably larger than the present St Paul's Cathedral. Closely packed buildings advanced to join with those clustered around the twin palaces of Westminster and Whitehall, Parliament and Westminster Abbey. South of the river lay the new suburb of Southwark, where the Globe, Swan and Rose theatres were located amidst London's red-light district, swarming with prostitutes, petty criminals and beggars, the lowlife that so fascinated the playwrights Ben Jonson and Robert Greene.

70

'At length they all to merry London come.' Edmund Spenser

THE RIVER THAMES AT RICHMOND
In this early 17th-century painting, the Royal Palace shows up clearly on the opposite bank. 'Sweet Thames, run softly, till I end my song,' wrote Elizabethan playwright Thomas Dekker.

The chronicler John Stow, who lived more than 80 years in London, mourned the continual loss of green fields, yet Chelsea, Paddington and Islington remained villages, and Queen Elizabeth could hunt foxes in open countryside where Oxford Street now stands – the distinctive cry of the hunters giving Soho its name. And not all the houses were cramped. The merchants' grand houses, full of newly introduced Tudor delights such as upholstered furniture, carpets and wallpaper, lined the Strand and ran down to the river. Out through Chelsea stretched the King's Road, Henry VIII's private route westwards to Hampton Court – in those days very much in the depth of the country.

AN ELIZABETHAN ENTREPRENEUR

By the middle of the 16th century there were so many merchants conducting business in Lombard Street that it became too congested for people to get through the street – a Tudor traffic jam! The enterprising Sir Thomas Gresham spotted a unique business opportunity and opened The Exchange, a purpose-built area for merchants to wheel and deal, a forerunner of today's Stock Exchange. On the upper galleries were more than 100 shops – the nation's first shopping mall! Queen Elizabeth bought her hats here and in 1571 awarded The Exchange its royal title.

'This city of London is so large and splendidly built, so populous and excellent in craft and merchant citizens, and so prosperous, that it is not only the first in the whole realm of England, but is esteemed one of the most famous in all Christendom,' commented Thomas Platter of Basle.

A HIDEOUS DEATH

A dramatic contemporary picture showing apparently naked witches being publicly burned at the stake at a market-place in Guernsey in the Channel Islands.

IN A VIOLENT AGE, the Tudors were tough on crime, any offence resulting in a far more severe punishment than today. Minor misdemeanours were punished by subjection to the ducking stool or by public humiliation in the stocks or pillory, where there was a real risk of losing an eye through being hit by a missile hurled by a jeering spectator. The 1572 Act for the Punishment of Vagabonds required 'all convicted vagabonds aged 14 or over to be whipped and burnt through the right ear.' Whipping posts were prominent throughout Tudor England.

When the Norfolk squire John Stubbs published a pamphlet that criticized Queen Elizabeth, his right hand was cut off outside Whitehall Palace. According to onlookers, Stubbs then doffed his hat with his left hand and cried, 'God save the Queen,' before being consigned to the Tower. Debtors were incarcerated in prisons like the Fleet, and convicted criminals could spend a lifetime amidst appalling conditions in Newgate.

More severe crimes meant execution at Tower Hill, Tyburn or similar public places. Justice had to be seen to be done – there was always a salutary row of heads displayed on spikes at London Bridge. Death came via the axe, dangling on a noose, or the particularly hideous fate of being hanged, drawn and quartered, whereby the victim was cut down from the gibbet whilst still alive, castrated, disembowelled, dismembered and then publicly displayed.

⌇

Torture continued to be widely used throughout the Tudor period. Confessions were extracted from prisoners by using a variety of appalling instruments, the most notorious being the rack, which few victims were able to resist. Mark Smeaton, a musician at Henry VIII's Court, was forced to confess to an affair with Anne Boleyn after being tortured on the rack. One of the most sadistic torturers was Richard Topcliffe, who during the latter half of the 16th century kept a range of torture instruments at his home which were reputedly more horrendous than those at the Tower of London.

⌇

Witchcraft became a capital offence in 1563, with those found guilty being burnt at the stake. This same form of the death penalty was also used for heretics, most notably in Mary's reign. The crime of breaking and entering with intent to steal was also judged sufficiently serious in the 16th century to be a capital offence. Crime definitely did not pay.

THE COURT OF THE STAR CHAMBER

King Henry VII established the Court of the Star Chamber in 1487 in order to speed up judicial procedures throughout his kingdom. Its name came from the star-shaped ceiling decoration of the room in the Palace of Westminster where meetings were first conducted. It continued to try both criminal and civil cases throughout the Tudor age and was finally abolished in 1641 during the reign of Charles I.

MEN OF LAW

Tudor judges in all their finery. The greatest judge of the age was Sir Edward Coke who was successively Solicitor General, Attorney General and Lord Chief Justice.

PENALTY FOR POVERTY

Vagabonds being flogged through the streets. They were an unwelcome cost to local authorities, who would try to move them out of the parish as quickly as possible.

FOOD AND CLOTHES

THE TUDORS LOVED eating. 'These English have their houses made of sticks and dirt, but they fare commonly well as the king,' noted a bemused Spaniard. Henry VIII had a massive appetite, as, it seems, did many of his subjects: even a labourer's breakfast could consist of bread, salted herring, cold meat, cheese and ale. A single course for a wealthier man's family supper might comprise 'nine joints of mutton, capon, four conies, two teals and a woodcock'. A well-laden table demonstrated wealth.

Fish was eaten on Fridays and during Lent, with a choice of stewed carp or pike, haddock, salmon, tench, ling, sturgeon or eel. Game included duck, partridge, pheasant, quail and woodcock, together with roasted blackbird, lark, sparrow, dove, swan or even peacock. Poor people's diet was generally restricted to broth, porridge, black rye bread, dairy produce and, sometimes, chicken or bacon. The rich regarded milk, butter, eggs and green vegetables as peasant food.

Although the medieval practice of gardening to provide food continued into the 16th century, these gardens often became more stylish and decorative, and can still be seen at many places such as Kenilworth Castle. The Tudors also designed gardens purely for pleasure with topiary and wonderfully patterned beds known as 'knots'. Most town dwellings had gardens for growing food and it was common practice to keep a pig – even in London!

FAMILY PORTRAIT

This portrait of Lord Cobham and his family hangs on the Grand Staircase at Longleat in Wiltshire. Cobham was Warden of the Cinque Ports and his wife was a lady-in-waiting to Queen Elizabeth.

Root crops were not widely cultivated in Tudor England, making it difficult to keep cattle over winter, so meat such as beef and mutton was salted or pickled, and seasoned with spices and sauces. Dovecotes and fishponds still featured prominently to maintain fresh food throughout winter. Choice increased as new products appeared from overseas. Turkeys and tobacco came from the New World and John Hawkins introduced potatoes in 1564. Only periodically did poor harvests create famine and shortages, when bread was made from acorns and belts tightened over large Tudor stomachs.

GOING TO MARKET

A country woman carries two pairs of geese and a hen to market. Tudor markets were important since permanent shops were not commonplace in 16th-century England.

TUDOR FASHION

The Tudors valued tradition and adored dressing up whatever the occasion. Those at Court spent fortunes on fashion. Elsewhere, those who had become successful could be equally flamboyant: **'The lawyers they go ruffling in their silks, velvets and chains of gold,'** noted a 16th-century follower of fashion. Furs and silks were favourite materials, purple a much-loved colour, together with masses of jewellery, embroidery and lace. Men postured in tightly padded doublet and hose, starched ruffs and extravagant hats. Women paraded in ruffs forming dramatic collars, their stiffened bodices flared out into enormous hooped skirts called farthingales. Further down the social scale, outfits were typically more conservative, the emphasis being on good quality cloth. At the bottom of society, clothing was of rough wool or cotton.

DEMURELY FASHIONABLE

Hans Holbein's portrait of a Tudor lady in contemporary dress with full skirt, coife and veil, and a rosary dangling from her waist.

WIVES AND MOTHERS

A TUDOR MARRIAGE WAS usually a carefully orchestrated affair, be it for monarch or commoner – a business arrangement to safeguard family fortunes, enhance wealth and property and advance social status. The bride was expected to provide an appropriately large dowry. Love matches and 'Romeo and Juliet' scenarios were strictly for the stage. The traditional Catholic Church considered marriage a necessary evil for those women too weak to remain virgins, whereas the Protestant Church regarded marriage as perfectly acceptable – providing the wife remained obedient to her husband!

Sex before marriage (and outside marriage) was illegal in Tudor times, which is possibly why Shakespeare was so quick to marry Anne Hathaway after she became pregnant. One reported method of birth control involved drinking honey-suckle juice for 37 consecutive days. Abortion was against the law – a woman faced execution if she was unable to prove her child had died of natural causes. Failure to conceive was always considered to be the responsibility of the wife. As a cure for this misfortune, women who were barren were advised to touch the hand of a hanged man.

A TUDOR FAMILY

A prosperous 16th-century family with husband and wife surrounded by dutiful children. A large joint of roast beef awaits, but note there are no vegetables on the table.

'Mr William Lewyn and I took order that Margaret Dutton should be first whipped at Gravesend and then sent to a house of correction for a bastard woman child there born.' An Elizabethan Justice of the Peace

TUDOR BABY

The infant Henry Unton with a wetnurse in attendance behind his crib. The picture, part of a montage of the life of Unton, Elizabeth's Ambassador to France, is in the National Portrait Gallery, London.

'HUBBLE BUBBLE, TOIL AND TROUBLE'

Shakespeare's dramatic account of Macbeth's encounter with the three witches encapsulates the Tudor attitude towards witchcraft. Superstition and fear were widespread during the 16th century, among people from farm labourers to churchmen. John Jewel, Bishop of Salisbury, implored Queen Elizabeth to revive the punitive laws against witches. Even he considered medical conditions now recognized as strokes or cancer to be the result of magic spells, cast by the servants of the Devil invoking supernatural powers to inflict harm on good, God-fearing Christians. Any unmarried woman who had the misfortune of attracting the notice of hostile or jealous neighbours might be accused of being a witch. Men meanwhile escaped being branded wizards and some, such as John Dee and Walter Raleigh, could dabble almost with impunity in what might be considered sorcery.

Motherhood remained a hazardous affair. Many women, including Jane Seymour and Catherine Parr, died in childbirth, probably through inadequate medical procedures and poor hygiene at the time of delivery. The traditional regard for the midwife's abilities declined in the Tudor era, due to the growing importance of male physicians, and the midwife's skill even became confused with witchcraft. As there was still no satisfactory substitute for breastfeeding, however, the wetnurse remained an essential part of a newborn baby's welfare.

Infant mortality was high – one third of all 16th-century children died in their first five years. Being either a mother or an infant during the Tudor age was fraught with difficulty.

GIVING BIRTH

Midwives assist a woman in labour using a birthing chair, considered in Tudor times a preferable delivery position to lying in bed. It was not thought appropriate for men to be in attendance at the birth.

TUDORS AT WORK

HARD AT WORK

In Tudor England there was a myriad of different jobs and trades, with most of the work done by hand.

TUDOR TOOLS

These carpenters' tools, which were found in the wreck of the Mary Rose, are now on display at the Portsmouth Dockyard together with many other artefacts from Henry VIII's flagship.

TUDOR WASHDAY

This colourful picture showing washerwomen at work in the open air appears in a manuscript dated 1589 which is now in the British Library, London.

CITIZENS OF TUDOR ENGLAND were astute, energetic and determined to succeed. Industry and commerce provided numerous new opportunities for advancement. Traditional agricultural practices were transformed due to improved husbandry, enclosure of common land, and the stimulus of providing food for rapidly expanding urban populations. New crops such as hops, turnips and potatoes were being introduced, but a rising European demand for English cloth meant that progressively more land was used for rearing sheep rather than growing crops.

SHEPHERDS AT WORK

A scene from The Book of Hours *by Simon Bening (1485–1561) conveys shepherds shearing sheep. The wool trade became progressively important during the Tudor era.*

The authorities became alarmed by the amount of woodland being felled to provide timber for greatly increased house construction, shipbuilding and for smelting in a developing iron industry. In response, coal mining grew eightfold between 1540 and 1640 in order to provide an alternative form of fuel, both for domestic and commercial purposes. Most 16th-century industry was concentrated in the Weald in Kent, East Anglia and the Cotswolds. The latter two regions were centres of cloth weaving, whereas the iron industry at that time was located in the Weald.

Trade with newly discovered overseas territories increased dramatically, dealing in exotic products like spices, gold, ivory and silk. John Hawkins and Francis Drake prospered from, among their other activities, slave trading from Africa and privateering on the Spanish Main. London was the centre of the most powerful guilds and livery companies. The Muscovy Company of Merchant Adventurers began to trade with Russia in 1553, and, at the end of the century, the formation of the East India Company paved the way for an overseas empire.

Nevertheless, unemployment was high in the second half of the century and there was no unemployment benefit; indeed those out of work could expect harsh treatment, particularly if classified as vagrants. Alternative ways of making a living did exist but could prove very hazardous.

Towards the end of the century, well over 100,000 men served in Elizabeth's armies on active service overseas in Ireland, France and the Netherlands. Pay was erratic and life expectancy short. The same was true of the queen's navy, yet even men as illustrious as John Donne volunteered for the Essex and Raleigh expedition against the Spanish in 1597. In Tudor times most people had little option but to take whatever work was available.

LIFE AND DEATH

LIFE IN TUDOR ENGLAND could seriously endanger your health – even monarchs were not exempt. Henry VIII was once thought to have syphilis but might well have been suffering from scurvy, a disease shared by sailors and the upper classes, perhaps because the latter believed that vegetables were fit only for the poor. Edward VI probably died of tuberculosis. Queen Mary is thought to have had ovarian cancer. Queen Elizabeth contracted smallpox, but recovered.

TUDOR DIAGNOSIS

A late 15th-century woodcut shows a doctor holding up a flask to the sun in order to examine a urine sample, while the patient looks on anxiously.

Malaria was rife amidst the mosquito-infested marshes of Essex and the Fens. Among venereal diseases, syphilis was as dangerous and as feared as Aids is today. Worst of all, however, was bubonic plague, which wiped out one sixth of the population of London in 1603. In the words of a contemporary ditty:

> *'Some streets had churches*
> *full of people weeping,*
> *some others had taverns*
> *rude revel keeping.'*

TUDOR CHEMIST

An apothecary surrounded by flasks of pills and potions, which he used to treat the ailments of his many customers. Today, Hall's Croft in Stratford-upon-Avon has a dispensary furnished as in the time of Shakespeare's son-in-law, Dr John Hall.

OUTBREAK OF PLAGUE

'The purple whip of vengeance, the plague, having beaten many thousands of men, women and children to death, and still marking the people of this city every week by the hundreds for the grave, is the only cause that all her inhabitants walk up and down like mourners at some great silent funeral.' This was Elizabethan poet Thomas Dekker's vivid description of the outbreak of the plague which struck London in 1593, one of several outbreaks that occurred during the reign of Henry VIII and again in Elizabeth's time: 17,000 citizens died in London in 1563 and 38,000 in the summer of 1603, when the plague delayed the entry of James I into London for his coronation. The artist Hans Holbein died of the plague in 1543 aged 45.

'If a man be sick of the plague then he sits and dies all alone.' *William Bridge, a Tudor preacher*

The average life expectancy in Tudor England was a mere 38 years.

Some remedies were weird and wondrous, such as drinking a powder of dried earthworms in broth made from a newt's tongue, or swallowing roasted onions filled with treacle and pepper. Diagnosis could be aided by examining urine according to the phases of the moon, or by using blood, phlegm and yellow bile. Amputations were cauterized with boiling oil and treacle, and a universal cure for virtually everything involved bloodletting with leeches. Remedies often seemed worse than the disease.

Physicians and surgeons vied for supremacy while looking down on apothecaries, to whom many people went for diagnoses as well as remedies. There was a great fear of 'quacks' stealing their business. After the dissolution of the monasteries, two of today's best-known London hospitals, St Bartholomew's and St Thomas's, were refounded in buildings that had hitherto been monastic properties. Previously many of the sick, particularly the less well off members of society, had relied on the monks to care for them.

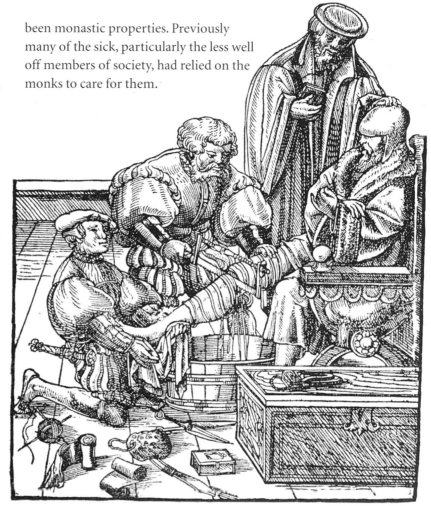

BRUTAL REMEDY
A woodcut showing a man having a leg amputated without the use of anaesthetics. Surgery in Tudor times was risky as well as painful.

THE KING'S CHARTER
This painting by Holbein shows Henry VIII handing over a charter to Thomas Vickary, his Chief Surgeon, at a gathering of the Guild of Barber Surgeons in 1541. The charter promoted the surgeons' standing within the community.

THE MODERN GLOBE THEATRE

An authentic replica of Shakespeare's Globe Theatre has been recreated in Southwark beside the River Thames. Plays are produced and performed here as in Shakespeare's day.

ENTER STAGE LEFT

An illustration from the British Library, London, shows travelling players arriving at a country manor house to perform before the owner and his guests.

HENRY VII'S COURT was noted for its interest in intellectual matters and the English Renaissance had its beginnings there. Both Henry VIII and his daughter Elizabeth I were well educated with a reverence for scholarship and a keen interest in the arts. Under their influence and encouragement a huge upsurge in learning and artistic activity took place.

The Renaissance had taken time to travel to England, and a full flowering of artistic achievement only took place during Elizabeth's reign. By that time England was firmly Protestant, making it a safe haven for people wishing to escape Catholic persecution on the Continent, and encouraging a number of skilled foreign painters to come to work in this country. Meanwhile the professional theatre, with actors performing in purpose-built, permanent buildings, was developing for the first time.

Education expanded, moving out of the sphere of the Church that had nurtured it as the country developed. Members of the new middle class now claimed the privileges formerly limited to the aristocracy. Enlightened and articulate 'new men', with university degrees and a sound public or grammar school education, rose to prominence. In turn such people became patrons of the arts, commissioning paintings, supporting the theatre and founding new colleges and schools.

A POPULAR SPORT

The cock-pit was purpose built for cockfighting. Large bets were placed leading to the ruin of many. Princess Elizabeth's tutor Roger Ascham, for example, was a compulsive gambler.

> '*Then the whining schoolboy, with his satchel and shining morning face, creeping like snail unwillingly to school.*'
>
> As You Like It,
> *William Shakespeare*

THE TUDOR AGE HERALDED a wider emphasis on education, with school sometimes followed by university. A sound legal training often led to political success and wealth, while literature was open even to those of humble origins. Christopher Marlowe's father was a cobbler, John Donne's an ironmonger, and Ben Jonson's stepfather was a bricklayer.

Tudor schoolboys worked long hours, from seven in the morning until five in the afternoon, six days a week. Holidays were much shorter than they are now, with just two weeks off at Christmas and at Easter. The main subject taught in Tudor schools was Latin, together with Greek, ancient history, religion and English. Discipline was strict, enforced by beatings: the motto of Louth Grammar School in Lincolnshire, founded in 1552, was 'Spare the rod and spoil the child'. Girls' education was generally thought to be less important than boys', although not all Tudor women remained uneducated.

WOLSEY'S
COLLEGE
Tom Quad at Christ Church, the largest college at Oxford University, originally founded as Cardinal's College by Cardinal Wolsey in 1525. Henry VIII later changed the name.

Public schools like St Paul's, Repton, Rugby and Harrow began in Tudor times, while the number of grammar schools increased considerably during Elizabeth's reign. Wolsey founded Christ Church at Oxford University, originally called

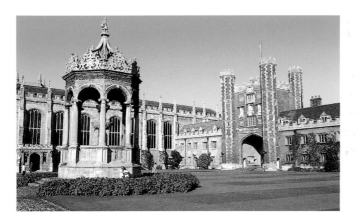

TRINITY COLLEGE, CAMBRIDGE

Trinity College was founded by Henry VIII, whose statue stands above the Great Gate. Archbishop Whitgift was once Master, Francis Bacon and the Earl of Essex were pupils.

Cardinal's College, and Henry VIII created Trinity College, Cambridge. Students entered university at a far earlier age – the Earl of Essex and Francis Bacon were only 12 when they enrolled at Trinity. Studies continued for up to six years and included logic, metaphysics, rhetoric, ethics, mathematics and physics. Theology, medicine and law were studied after attaining a first degree. The best of Tudor education was available even to the poor. A student could enter university as a sizar, receiving a free education by serving at table, cleaning boots and performing other menial tasks. Isaac Newton was a sizar at Trinity, Cambridge.

TUDOR GRAMMAR SCHOOL

The schoolroom at Stratford-upon-Avon where it is claimed that Shakespeare was taught. The wooden desks are 19th century, but otherwise the room is much as Shakespeare might have known it.

THE TYNDALE BIBLE

One of the most remarkable scholars of the Tudor era was William Tyndale, who translated the New Testament of the Bible into English. In 1524, having failed to find support for his work in England, Tyndale moved to the Continent. There he published his Bible as well as writings promoting Protestantism. These activities brought him to the attention of the Catholic authorities, who convicted him of heresy and burned him at the stake in Antwerp in 1536. Three years later, King Henry VIII ordered that a copy of the English Bible should be placed in every church throughout the land. Not everyone approved: 'I have never read the Scripture nor never will read it,' stated the Duke of Norfolk. Yet Tyndale's translation, from the Greek and Hebrew, shows fine scholarship and great literary skill. It was a sure foundation for later translations, and sections survive word for word in the King James Bible of 1611.

SCHOLARLY MEMORIAL
A memorial to William Tyndale at North Nibley in the Cotswolds. Miles Coverdale, who also translated the New Testament, came from this part of England, too.

TUDORS AT PLAY

FÊTE AT BERMONDSEY

The 16th-century artist George Hoefnagel graphically portrays Elizabethan life in his painting which now hangs in Hatfield House in Hertfordshire.

'SOMETIMES THEIR NECKS ARE broken, sometimes their backs, sometimes their legs, sometimes their arms' – not a description of some brutal medieval torture, but of 16th-century football. This sport was hugely popular, especially on occasions such as Shrove Tuesday and Ascension Day when entire villages played each other in all-day encounters, the object being to capture the ball and bring it back to their own village. The authorities frowned on football, thinking that it diverted the villagers from archery, a far more useful recreation which practised military skills.

Higher up the social order, jousting could be equally robust. Huge crowds of ordinary folk paid to watch handsome young Henry VIII and later the charismatic Earl of Essex, although by this time jousting had become more of a colourful pageant than a mock-military encounter. The gentry hunted deer, practised falconry and played bowls – even, as legend has it, as the Armada approached.

The Tudors developed lawns largely for the purpose of playing bowls. 'My lord under a tree ... walks with a book in his

MARKETS AND FAIRS

The traditional weekly market was both business enterprise and social occasion, somewhere to purchase a wide variety of goods, meet friends and exchange the latest gossip. The annual fairs lasted two weeks or more, the most famous of them being at St Bartholomews at Smithfield in London and Stourbridge near Cambridge. Traders and customers came from far and wide. There were wrestlers, jugglers, minstrels, fortune-tellers, dancing bears and all manner of entertainment.

REAL GAME OF TENNIS
A 16th-century engraving shows real, or royal, tennis, an indoor-forerunner of lawn tennis. The royal tennis court at Hampton Court is still used regularly.

In Tudor times, people at every level in society knew how to enjoy themselves. Christmas celebrations lasted 12 days, a time when the lord of the manor entertained not only wealthy friends but also the village poor, with feasting, singing, dancing and plenty of games. Dancing was particularly popular, enjoyed equally at Court and around the village maypole.

Music was very important throughout Tudor society. King Henry VIII and Queen Elizabeth were both skilled instrumentalists and Francis Drake employed a string quartet aboard the *Golden Hind* during his historic round-the-world voyage. All over England any skilled fiddler was always in great demand and could command large sums of money to perform at village gatherings.

hand to keep him from sleeping and we ready with bowls, but the weather somewhat too warm yet,' wrote one of Lord Burghley's retainers. Pall-mall, a form of croquet, was also played on grass. Other gentle activities included board games and cards, such as whist which was invented in Tudor times. According to the playwright Ben Jonson, Queen Elizabeth cheated at cards – like most Tudors she took games seriously and always played to win.

ELIZABETHAN ALFRESCO
An elaborate 16th-century picnic, with music provided by a trio of colourful musicians. Feast days were a regular feature in Tudor England, celebrated by all levels of society.

A MAJOR FEATURE OF the Tudor age was the growth of the performing arts, particularly theatre, which evolved from miracle and mystery plays via travelling players to culminate in the purpose-built playhouses of Queen Elizabeth's reign.

Mystery plays, based on biblical stories, are still performed in York and have been revived at Chester. The appearance of travelling players at Stratford-upon-Avon is said to have inspired Shakespeare's theatrical career. Playhouses, such as the Swan, the Rose and the Globe on the South Bank of the River Thames in London, developed from the courtyards of coaching inns where hitherto plays had been performed.

The original Globe Theatre was destroyed when a spark from a cannon, fired during a performance, set fire to the thatched roof and burned the theatre to the ground. A spectator had his breeches set ablaze but was saved by being doused with a bottle of beer. Sam Wanamaker, the American actor and director, inspired an authentic replica to be built on a site beside the Thames, and today plays are performed there as in Shakespeare's day.

Theatre was the cinema of the day, appealing as much to the man in the street as to the intellectual or noble lord. Actors such as Richard Burbage, Ned Alleyn and William Kempe became its first stars. Women were not allowed on stage – there were no Nell Gwynnes in Tudor theatre – so the female roles were played by boys. When a French company performed a play which featured actresses in London towards the end of the 16th century, they were booed off the stage.

A different play was staged every afternoon, generating enormous demand for works from talented playwrights such as William Shakespeare, Ben Jonson and Christopher Marlowe. Often plays were created by groups of writers, just like some present-day television shows.

Theatres were packed. Ordinary folk were called 'groundlings' because they stood in the open air in front of the stage in an area known as the yard, whilst richer patrons

> *'Sweet speeches, comedies and pleasing shows.'*
>
> Christopher Marlowe

PORTRAIT OF A TUDOR PLAYWRIGHT

This painting is believed to be of the Elizabethan playwright Christopher Marlowe. He was a dramatist of considerable talent, but died at the young age of 29, reputedly as a result of becoming embroiled in a tavern brawl in Deptford, London.

SHAKESPEARE'S FELLOW DRAMATISTS

Christopher Marlowe's *Edward II*, *Tamburlaine the Great* and *The Tragicall History of Doctor Faustus* were all works of great power and poetry and his premature death was a major loss to English drama. Ben Jonson, another leading dramatist of the day, was a close companion of Shakespeare. Although better educated than Shakespeare, Jonson was less prolific.

A PRIVATE PERFORMANCE

Players perform a masque at a private banquet. Shakespeare's later work was much influenced by the masque form, while fellow playwright Ben Jonson created numerous masques with Inigo Jones providing the sets.

ONCE A TUDOR THEATRE

The George Inn at Southwark in London is now owned by The National Trust. The galleried courtyard provided a natural theatre in the mid-16th century.

sat above in covered galleries and were nicknamed 'the gods'. Groundlings were both enthusiastic and knowledgeable, yet could be highly critical. If a play was to succeed it was essential to capture their interest at the outset. With profound insight into human nature, powerful words and storyline, Shakespeare certainly could.

WILLIAM KEMPE DANCING

One of the outstanding actors of the day, Kempe reputedly once danced all the way from London to Norwich.

WILLIAM SHAKESPEARE

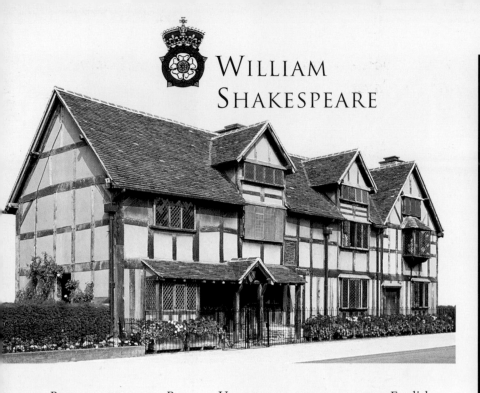

BIRTHPLACE OF THE BARD

John Shakespeare's house at Stratford-upon-Avon, where the English nation's most famous playwright was born on 23 April 1564.

UNQUESTIONABLY THE GREATEST English dramatist, William Shakespeare has been admired for more than four centuries. No other writer's body of work comes near to matching the richness, humanity and vitality present in his plays and poems and no other single person has ever made such an important contribution to the English language.

THE FACE OF GENIUS

The 'Flower' portrait of William Shakespeare is in the Royal Shakespeare Theatre Gallery at Stratford-upon-Avon. It was presented by Mrs Charles Flower in 1895.

Born in Stratford-upon-Avon, the son of a glove maker who was a member of the town corporation, Shakespeare was educated at the local grammar school. At the age of 18, he married the pregnant Anne Hathaway. The financial pressure of keeping a wife and three young children may well have led him, a few years later, to join one of the London acting companies which visited Stratford in the 1580s.

MACBETH MEETS THE THREE WITCHES

Shakespeare derived themes from stories already in general circulation, in this case Holinshed's Chronicles of England, Scotlande, and Irelande.

Success in the capital came quickly. By 1593 Shakespeare had written seven well-received plays, including *Richard III*, *The Taming of the Shrew* and *Titus Andronicus*. Royal favour counted for a great deal in Tudor London. Shakespeare's later company, The Lord Chamberlain's Men, played regularly at Elizabeth's Court. His output was prodigious: *Henry V*, *Much Ado About Nothing* and *Julius Caesar* were all conceived in a single year; his works ranged from the riotous comedy of *Twelfth Night* to the shimmering imagery of *The Tempest* and the sinister sense of impending doom in *Macbeth*.

By 1597 Shakespeare was wealthy enough to buy a large house in Stratford, where he became an increasingly important figure and to where he finally retired in 1612. He died here four years later, after, it is said, 'a too merry meeting' during a visit from Ben Jonson and poet Michael Drayton, and was buried in the parish church where he had been baptized.

COINING A WELL-TURNED PHRASE

These are a few of the words and phrases that Shakespeare introduced into the English language:

bated breath

bloodstained

to cater

downstairs

flesh and blood

one fell swoop

spotless reputation

uncomfortable

the world is your oyster

'All the world's a stage, And all the men and women merely players.'

As You Like It, *William Shakespeare*

THE GLOBE THEATRE
Built by the impressario Richard Burbage in 1599, with Shakespeare as part owner, the Globe was situated in Southwark in an area full of gambling dens and brothels. One of the first plays to be performed there was Shakespeare's Julius Caesar.

ART AND MUSIC

THE VISUAL ARTS REACHED new heights in England when the Renaissance came to these shores. Previously the English Church had lacked the funds of the Vatican and English monarchs had rarely been culturally inclined. Artists were regarded as craftsmen, architecture merely a craft supervised by the master mason. Then Henry VIII and Elizabeth changed all this.

The new king saw himself as a man of many talents, including the arts, and had himself painted by Hans Holbein on many occasions. In turn, Elizabeth liked to be painted to further the royal image, resulting in such fine works of art as George Gower's 'Armada' portrait, Robert Peake's celebrated *Procession to Blackfriars* and William Segar's 'Ermine' portrait.

GLORIANA

The so-called 'Ermine' portrait of Elizabeth, painted by William Segar and commissioned by Sir Robert Cecil, is full of imagery and the complex symbolism so beloved by the Elizabethans. It can be seen at Hatfield House in Hertfordshire.

Artistic asylum-seekers, among them Marcus Gheeraerts, Isaac Oliver and John de Critz, came to Elizabethan England to escape religious oppression on the European mainland. Gheeraerts introduced painting on canvas to the English nation, quickly becoming the leading Tudor portrait artist by painting fashionable ladies of the Court in a flattering light. Gheeraerts also created those classic images of Queen Elizabeth, *The Rainbow Portrait* and *The Ditchley Portrait.*

At the same time the miniature portrait became popular. Courtiers wore a picture of the queen as a badge, in this way demonstrating loyalty and devotion for all to see. Devon-born Nicholas Hilliard became the leading exponent of the miniature and achieved international recognition for his exquisitely detailed works. Today some of the best of Tudor painting can be seen in the National Portrait Gallery in London.

The Tudors used their patronage of the the arts to flaunt their wealth and enhance their cultural credentials, commissioning an eminent artist to paint their portrait or an inspiring architect to create an impressive showhouse. Roger Smythson was the leading architect of the day, responsible for Longleat, Hardwick Hall and Wollaton Hall, a trio of exuberant magnificence where Smythson skilfully blended the principles of the Renaissance with those of the High Perpendicular, the final phase of Gothic architecture. It was left to a young Elizabethan theatre set designer, Inigo Jones, to introduce Palladianism from Italy, but not until the 1620s – Tudor taste was not ready for such a radically different architectural style.

Both Henry and Elizabeth were particularly fond of music. Henry composed some music of his own. William Byrd and Thomas Tallis benefited greatly from the queen's patronage. Byrd is regarded as the father of the English keyboard and with Tallis began the strong tradition of English choral music which still exists today. Elizabeth's organist, John Bull, composed *God Save the Queen.*

This wealth of artistic achievement, allied to the consummate skill of Tudor poets and playwrights, ensured that England finally emerged to join the great cultural revolution that had spread across Europe from Renaissance Italy.

PERFECT MINIATURE

Nicholas Hilliard's A young man leaning against a tree among roses, *in the Victorian and Albert Museum, is said to portray the Earl of Essex. It represents a fine example of the art of 'limning'.*

'NO MAN IS AN ISLAND …'

So wrote the metaphysical poet John Donne, who later became Dean of St Paul's Cathedral. Donne wrote many love poems and sonnets as well as a series of holy sonnets.

ON GUARD!

Henry VII introduced the first permanent troops, named The Yeomen of the Guard. Today they reside at the Tower of London and are more popularly known as Beefeaters.

'THUS FROM SMALL THINGS to great things.' The inscription on Drake's Drum at Buckland Abbey, his one-time South Devon home, encapsulates the spirit of the Tudor age. The 116-year-span of Tudor rule witnessed momentous events which were to have a profound influence on subsequent generations. America had been discovered. Drake had circumnavigated the globe. The defeat of the Spanish Armada had saved the Tudor kingdom and established it as a maritime power.

Shakespeare, Marlowe, Donne and other hugely talented writers had initiated England's lasting reputation as a literary nation. England had embraced Protestantism and the Anglican Church was firmly established. Musket and cannon had irrevocably superseded longbow and siege engine. A full-time navy had been established. The rule of law and justice was firmly woven into the social fabric of the nation. Members of a rapidly growing middle class rose to prominence. Parliament had begun to establish itself as a powerful voice, ignored by monarchs at their peril – as the Stuart kings were later to discovered.

Colonization of newly discovered territories began during Elizabeth's reign. Raleigh had pioneered Virginia, the first English colony on the North American mainland. Towards the end of the Tudor age, the establishment of the East India Company was the seed from which grew an overseas empire that would cover a quarter of the globe and whose present-day legacy is the Commonwealth.

The Tudor era was a defining period of English history, a time during which the nation was transformed from a loose-knit medieval kingdom of no particular consequence into a highly centralized modern state, a powerful and prosperous nation with a sense of pride, purpose and self belief. The Tudor monarchs, particularly Henry VIII, the first English ruler to be addressed as 'your majesty', and his daughter Elizabeth, revered virtually as a goddess in her lifetime, continue to be a source of fascination to the present day.

INDEX